SISTERFRIENDS

EMPOWERMENT FOR WOMEN AND A CELEBRATION OF SISTERHOOD

BY

JEWEL DIAMOND TAYLOR

Quiet Time Publishing
P.O. Box 10366
Marina del Rey, CA 90295

Copyright © 1998 by Jewel Diamond Taylor

ISBN: 1884743-064

Library of Congress Catalog Card Number: 97-67877
Taylor, Jewel   CIP
        Sisterfriends
        Empowerment For Women And A Celebration Of Sisterhood

Editor: Marcie Eanes
Cover Photographer: Byron Nickleberry
Cover Design: Natalie Robinson

Quiet Time Publishing
P.O. Box 10366
Marina del Rey, CA 90295
E-mail: QTPublish@aol.com

12 11 10 9 8 7 6 5 4 3 2 1

This book is dedicated to the women and sisterfriends who have loved me and "held me up on every leaning side." These women are the jewels in my crown.

In Memory of....
My mother - Lyn Hudson
My aunt - Janet Parker
You will always be remembered

READ

by
Jewel Diamond Taylor

Read so you can think well.

Read so you can write well.

Read so you can speak well.

Read to expand your mind.

Read instead of watching TV,
       it's a better use of your time.

Read about other people and places.

You'll meet and read about folk

just like you and some new faces.

Reading builds your confidence and knowledge.

Read and maybe, one day, you will write your own book.

Read for the joy it gives by traveling in history or
       to far places.

Anything you want to know is in a book

Just take a look.

Use your library....and your library card.

Support your neighborhood African-American owned
       book stores.

Read books by African-American authors.

Read so you can succeed.

Read so you can lead.

READ and you shall RISE!

Contents

Acknowledgments

This book is a collaborative effort. Thank you God and to all the sisterfriends who made contributions. If you would like to contact any of our contributing writers, please see the appendix in the back of the book.

Thank you to my family, husband John, sons John and Jason, Joy and Neil Anderson, Jamilia Harold, Ronald Burton, Dr. David Horne, and Dr. Cornelia Lyles-Horne for your love, support and investments in this endeavor.

Special thanks to Iyanla Vanzant and Tracy Kennedy for your continuous support and encouragement. Thank you Deborah Granger, Quiet Time Publishing, for your commitment, sacrifice and believing in me. With the help of God, you made it possible for my words to come alive in this book and our previous project "Success Gems."

Thank you Maria Denise Dowd, Executive Producer of the African-American Women on Tour Conference. I'm forever grateful for the opportunity to work, travel and grow with you.

Special thanks to all my sisterfriends in my Enlightened Circle Motivational Support Network.

Introduction

Sister, my sister, where have you been? I've really missed you. I've seen you in the market, in malls, at work and even stood next to you in line at the bank and at times we didn't speak or even acknowledge each other.

Oh, I know you've been busy working that job, trying to be with your man, raise your children, balance your check book and keep up with the latest styles, taking care of aging parents or even going back to school yourself. I haven't seen much of you. We don't seem to have time to invite each other over to just sit and talk anymore.

We come home so tired from work. We don't even have time for ourselves. Oh, I know how choir rehearsal, committee meetings, homework, pagers, diapers, demands, TV, homes that need cleaning and cars that need fixin' keep us apart. But sisterfriend, we need to see each other more so we don't become so isolated and depressed.

9

Think about it my sisterfriend, when we get together we have a chance to laugh, share our stories, hug, cry, learn, bond, uplift one another and regroup. Don't cheat yourself. Treat yourself more often to sister support groups, retreats, book clubs, conferences or just visit and call a sister, save a sister from misery, loneliness and isolation.

Let's promise to be more accessible, sensitive and respect each other. So many of us are entrepreneurs. Let's network more and really do business with one another. Let's share more about how to parent our children, and how to keep a career and relationship at the same time. Let's talk more about being "change agents" in our community. Let's talk more about our spiritual joy and how God has "brought us through and not the things He didn't do." Let's talk more about our mothers, grandmothers and aunties with honor. Let's remember their struggles, sacrifices and successes, since we are now the mothers, aunties and grandmothers.

My sisterfriend, whether you are young, mature, hurting, strong, nubian, crystal black or light skin, creative, wounded, faith-filled, Christian, Muslim, Buddhist, Metaphysical, Catholic, AME, PhD, VIP, MD, AKA, NAACP, LINKS, entrepreneur, healer, administrator, married, single, divorced, student, homemaker, African-American, Carribean, musician, artist, designer, writer, educator, law enforcer, politician, or community activist....don't let labels, men, hairstyles, status, religion, racism or crowded agendas keep us apart. You are beautiful, divine, worthy and successful just as you are. As enlightened women we cannot afford to compare or compete.

It's time to heal our broken pieces. The pages within are a gift to you from myself and many sisterfriends. We are offering ideas, strategies, experience and testimonies. A community of sweet voices from your sistahs will share *soul*utions for successful living.

This book is comprised of the voices and experiences of other sisterfreinds and one brotherfriend. I felt it would be so much more balanced, inspiring and richer to invite the testimonies, wisdom and insight of others. It should read and feel like one long letter. Visualize yourself sitting around the table with me and the voices you will meet in the pages to follow. It's casual, open, caring and fun. We may cry, hug or exhale as we are talking and learning together, but it's OKAY. We all want to heal and grow. There are no egos at the table. We are sitting together sharing to help each other, inspiring each other and honoring each other. We are co-journers on the journey of life.

On your journey of life right now, you have this book in your hands. Our souls are meeting at an intersection, a crossroad. You may stay here a while to bask in this female sunshine of ideas and then move on to another path of discovery. Or you may linger a while to be nurtured by the sistahs as we become co-journers seeking the answers to life that bring wisdom and balance.

I reflect often on the story and movie of the Wizard of Oz. I find so many hidden messages within this childhood story of Dorothy's journey to find someone to help her find her way home again.

In the past I had given my power away so many times looking for something outside of myself to make me happy, to tell me what, when and how to do something or simply failed to listen to my own inner voice. As I began to heal my broken pieces, dissolve illusions, become spiritually aware and develop self-esteem, the subliminal message of Dorothy's journey to Oz became clear and relevant in my life.

Your life's journey may bring divorce, illness, loss of a loved one, loss of a job, a broken heart or financial setback which can cause you to feel lost and off-centered like the character Dorothy. When Dorothy realized she was lost, the "Good Witch" (Spirit's voice within) directed her to follow the yellow brick road. In other words, she was being guided to follow her own gut feeling, tap into her higher mind to know what to do to find her way to Emerald City. The color yellow symbolizes the golden light of awareness, clarity, concentration and creativity. The power of the Sun in our own sun center - the solar plexus - which influences our physical and mental well-being. The vibratory energy of yellow vitalizes and accelerates our mental strength. Yellow is the symbol of mind, intellect, high intelligence and wisdom. It is a positive, magnetic vibration that has a tonic effect on the nerves. Yellow is a great equalizer for irritable conditions of the nervous system. The word "soul" comes from sol or sun. The color yellow correlates to the light center within your being. Your third energy chakra is located by your navel and is the center of your body.

As Dorothy followed the yellow brick road she met three differenct characters (Scarecrow, Lion and Tin Man) who asked to accompany her on her journey to wholeness. Each character symbolizes the three most critical characteristics we need to be successful in life. The Scarecrow was seeking brains. The Lion wanted to stop being afraid. The Tin Man felt incomplete without a heart.

And so it is with our lives, we need knowledge, courage and love. Without these three attributes we fall prey to ignorance, fear, pain, low self-esteem, mistakes, and misery (the wicked witch). Also, she had her loyal and loving companion, a dog called To-To. Look at the word "dog" spelled backwards, it spells GOD. We need the unconditional loving companionship of God on our journey.

Along the way she was haunted, distracted and tempted by the "Bad Witch" and of course, the lions, tigers and bears. They represent the negative forces that try to steal your joy like negative people, negative habits or those temporary setbacks in your life. Dorothy even fell asleep for a while in a bed of poppy flowers. Sometimes we "fall asleep" on our journey. We get overwhelmed, off track, confused and just distracted with less important things.

After more challenges to overcome, Dorothy finally made it to the Emerald City. Green vibrates with harmony, health, nature and abundance. Green is the merging of yellow (soul) and blue (spirit). It appears in the spectrum at the point of color balance, between the first three rays (which are concerned with the physical aspect) and the last three rays (which relate to the spiritual aspect). Green reaches outward in a horizontal manner, blue reaches upward in a vertical manner. Together they form the cross which is a symbol of life.

Green relates to the heart energy field in your body. Green is calming and soothing to the nervous system. In Egypt and in the Orient, the emerald is believed to have wonderful curative properties for the eyes and was worn to protect against the evil eye. The emerald gem is a symbol of regeneration and life. It represents new birth and the development of a revitalized and beautiful physical body.

When Dorothy arrives in the Emerald City she is groomed, pampered, refreshed and prepared to meet the Oz. Oz is supposed to have the power to send her home. As the story unfolds Dorothy discovers the illusion of false power outside of herself. She finds out Oz is a fake and is told by the Good Witch that she had the power all along to go home. However, Dorothy had lessons to learn. Since she had the constant companionship of her dog (unconditional love) and her character(istics) of courage, love and wisdom, she was ready. All she had to do was put on the red ruby slippers.

The color red symbolizes life, energy, activity, blood, stimulating and invigorating the body. The focus is on her feet because the feet represent under*standing*. When she clicks her heels three times (mind, body and spirit....the trinity), she is becoming whole in her consciousness and understanding to stand tall in truth. This act of faith symbolizes breaking all illusions that someone outside of herself has power. Dorothy's new awareness of friends (courage, love and wisdom) empowers her wherever she goes. Her understanding is strong, clear and within. The prodigal daughter Dorothy can now go home.

Sisters, you and I are like Dorothy. We need to invite courage, love and wisdom into our lives and always commune with God. We too, can break the spell of illusions that someone or something is blocking our goodness or has the power to make us happy. We must improve our awareness and understanding about life's journey. As your understanding becomes stronger, so does your faith, self-esteem and ability to succeed.

On your yellow brick journey, I offer these pages as a map for reference to enrich, encourage, educate and enlighten your way to the Emerald City. Don't lose your ruby slippers or give your power away.

Your power, potential and *soul*utions are already within. You have a mind, body and Spirit....so click your heels three times....and Stay in the Light.

Jewel Diamond Taylor

FRIENDSHIP IS...

A priceless gift that cannot be bought or sold
but its' value is far greater than a mountain made of gold.
For gold is cold and lifeless
it can neither see nor hear
and in the time of trouble
gold is powerless to cheer
it has no ears to listen
no heart to understand
it cannot bring you comfort
or reach out a helping hand.
So when you ask God for a gift
be thankful if He sends
not diamonds, pearls or riches
but the love of real true Sisterfriends.

1

WHAT IS A SISTERFRIEND....

She sends greetings cards and letters to stay in touch even when you are miles away; she'll babysit for you so you won't miss that important class or meeting; she'll visit or give you a break from being homebound all the time taking care of an aging, sick parent, small children or a child with special physical needs; she calls you up just to see how you're feeling because she intuitively feels you are lonely.

She goes shopping with you looking for that special outfit to wear at your daughter's wedding; she listens to your poetry; she helps you paint the bedroom for the new baby arriving; she helps you address your wedding invitations; she listens to you talk about every little detail about that date; she supports you when you start your business when everyone else thinks you're crazy; she picks you up to go to the movies so you'll take a break from working all the time.

She goes on vacation with you; she remembers your birthday; she's the one who brings you a new night gown and book to read when you're sick or healing from an operation; she offers her name as a reference for your resume; she can stand for hours with you reading cards in a greeting card store; she'll attend your "pity party" each time you break up with a boyfriend or go through that divorce; she listens to you talk about the crazy people in your family.

During financial lean times, she makes sure you and the kids always have food in the refrigerator; she's by your side every day as a shoulder to cry on, an ear to listen, answers the phone and a helping hand when you're faced with the death of a loved one.

She knows your favorite color; when she finds something on sale, she buys one for you….and one for her; you share secrets that remain a secret; she doesn't dwell on your past mistakes or present shortcomings; you feel safe with her to be yourself, she doesn't take it personal and become over sensitive when you are being quiet or moody.

She's still around even when you are unpredictable, dramatic or corny; you may not even like each other's kids or mates, but you always make time for each other to laugh, reminisce, catch up and enjoy your special bond; she convinces you to treat yourself and buy something for yourself every once in a while....she says, "go ahead and buy that girl, you deserve it;" when the two of you go to restaurants, you don't keep track of every dollar spent, whoever <u>can</u> pay, pays.

She volunteers to help you with your special project; she listens to you complain about your Mother and how she still treats you like a child and tries to control you; she can make you laugh when you'd rather cry; she can relate to those good old days when you used to party and act a fool, she doesn't hold it against you; she's <u>genuinely excited</u> for you when you achieve a goal (graduation, buy a new home, get a new car, lose weight, get a promotion, stay sober and clean).

She sees qualities in you that you don't even see or believe; she doesn't give up on you easily or allow you to give up....or beat up on yourself; she calls you all the time even if she just talked to you yesterday; she encourages you to follow your dreams; she'll take you to the store, work or the doctor when your car breaks down; she'll remind you of your self-worth, beauty, strength and inner power to choose another path when you're being abused.

She prays with you; she sincerely cares about the welfare of other women; she's involved in positive outreach activities; she doesn't stand by and support any self-destructive behavior in her sisterfriend; she is a protector and nurturer of children; she is a faith walker and a positive talker; her laughter, hugs and conversation are always welcome because she is a "lifter" not a "leaner."

She takes time to reach out to sisters who are feeling depressed; she shares her testimony of endurance and faith; she sees beyond color, economic status, hair, labels, clothes, sins of the past and ego trips….she sees, loves, respects, listens, trusts and befriends her sister.

2

STEPPING OUT ON FAITH: I LEFT MY COMFORT ZONE

In 1985 I made a decision that would ultimately change my life 360 degrees. I kept thinking, dreaming and talking about a goal. I soon realized that "talk is cheap and I had to leap." So I wrote down my goals and a target date to leave my comfortable yet unfulfilling job of seven years.

I stepped out on faith two weeks before my target date. I left a very secure - paid every Friday - credit union - health insurance - paid Christmas holidays and a free turkey gift card - good paying job to become a motivational speaker.

Co-workers and certain family members thought I was crazy (and probably still do). Why would I leave a comfort zone, friends, a predictable routine, benefits, pleasant environment and a steady paycheck to step out into the unknown? I was going where no one I knew had gone before. There I was, a young African-American woman who never wrote a book, never attended a Toastmasters meeting and without a mentor, daring to enter a field that is dominated by white males. I believe that success and fulfillment come to us either because of a *choice, coincidence* or it's a *calling*. For me, it was a choice that answered an inner/higher call. We often call God…."something told me." Well, "SOMETHING told me" to let go of my job in the aerospace industry in 1985. Looking back, I now know I could have made a better transition to minimize some of the challenges. My experiences have been bittersweet. Yet, my rewards have far outweighed my regrets.

In life, some bridges we must cross and some we have to burn. Letting go meant I was burning a bridge. There was no turning back. This risk-taking, faith-walking, dare-to-dream, bridge-burning, dauntless behavior isn't recommended for everyone. But I'm designed that way. I call it my "holy boldness." I had a quiet sense of confidence, sense of urgency, determination, "I gotta go or I'll die" attitude rising up in me to grow and go. When that push is on your back so strong, you see what others can't see. You feel what can't be explained. You act in ways that can't be justified. You then are no longer seeking happiness but….fulfillment.

I had no idea what to expect. I just knew it was my time. I felt a strong tugging on my soul to leap. Even though I wasn't as spiritually grounded in my faith as I am now, somehow I knew that the voice of "Something told me" would lead me and not let me **fail**. I didn't say the voice of God wouldn't let me *fall*, because I fell many times on my journey of growth in a new career. However, I got up and attempted to learn the lesson, but I never *failed*.

Leaving a comfort zone and taking a leap of faith is scary and exhilarating at the same time. Self-empowerment and change happens when you make a decision and you remain committed to see it through *all the way*. New experiences require that you be alert, take calculated risks, be creative, open minded, and flexible.

My heart was pumping with adrenaline, anticipation and anxiety. I made THE decision. I set and met my target date. I began working part-time at various jobs for my "bread and butter" and part-time on the weekends as a speaker. But I still kept "the main thing....the MAIN THING."

My messages were on topics of self-esteem, goalsetting, parenting, spiritual joy and positive coping skills for life. I started with local YWCAs, church groups, recovery centers, teen mother groups, sales groups and community based organizations.

I landed on my feet after taking my leap of faith. My *choice* and my *calling* have enriched my life with international travel, TV and radio appearances, new friends, speaking engagements at government agencies, sales/marketing groups, universities, churches, hospitals, conferences, and retreats.

My faith leap introduced me to places and faces of the strong, the wounded, the celebrated, the corporate, the student, the entrepreneur, other speakers and authors. My books and tapes have been purchased by thousands of satisfied seekers of knowledge. The quality of life for me and my family is enriched because I am more fulfilled doing what I love.

I know that I am still committed and excited about my choice and my calling. I can cope with setbacks, tragedy and disappointments because I'm learning to practice what I preach. Faith, action, hard work, love, and self-correction are the guiding forces in my life. My speaking invitations, travel, income and opportunities grew as *I grew*. I've *gained* more than I have ever given. The transition of going from a steady paycheck to unpredictable and sometimes lean financial times deepened my faith and trust in God's abundant ability to meet all my needs.

What great experiences of growth and glory are you missing? Are you waiting for all the green lights to go? God is trying to tell you something. But maybe you lack trust in yourself, your intuition, your talents or even God. The affirmation I repeat when feeling unsure is "I am *led* and *fed* by the Spirit."

Don't let your dreams and goals grow cold. Don't let everyone "breath" on your baby. You see, your dream is like a brand new baby. You don't want everyone breathing on your baby, passing along their germs or saying it's an ugly baby. It's your baby, protect it, nurture it. Don't you think your baby is the prettiest baby? Don't let others pass judgement, define limitations or talk about past mistakes. Your dream/goal is a birthing process. You will have stretch marks and labor pains, but no one wants to hear about them. They just want you to show them the baby....the results. Everyone may not think your dream is so beautiful. So you must feel worthy and love your dream/goal. This is called your *passion.*

There are three categories of people who you should share your dream or goal. Either tell (1) *NOBODY*....It's too soon. Wait until you're strong, committed, and unwavering. If you hear any negative feedback, you might give up and backslide. (2) *SOMEBODY*....Maybe select people that you know are supportive, sincere, helpful and acknowledge your potential. (3) *EVERYBODY*....There are some goals you need to tell everyone because you never know where your blessing will come from. It usually comes from the least expected places and people. God is your *Source* but people are your *resources.* Allow others to help you. You don't have to re-invent the wheel.

You'll learn from your mistakes, but also learn from mentors, elders, classes, referrals, books, etc., to get closer to your goal.

3

A LITTLE BIT OF MONEY AND A LOT OF FAITH: HOW A SISTER TURNED HER PASSION INTO PROFIT

The first time I heard the endearment term "sisterfriend" was in 1991 when I attended and participated as the Mistress of Ceremonies for the African-American Women's Conference in San Diego.

I can truly say that attending that soul-full event was a turning point in my life. Then, and every year since, the conference has been on tour throughout the nation. I have experienced black-on-black love from sistahs that have empowered me. Today, my cultural celebration is now an everyday experience. My phone book and my "soul-o-dex" has changed. Speaking engagements and networking contacts have soared to another level. From city to city I meet dynamic, creative, spiritual, loving, caring, professional women on a mission.

Every year the executive producer of this empowerment conference, Marie Denise Dowd, has honored me to be the

Mistress of Ceremonies and speaker. I am her senior in years, yet I often tell her I want to be just like her when I grow up. She is the Founder/Executive Producer of African American Women on Tour and is my mentor by example, action, friendship and leaps of faith. I have witnessed her growth, professionalism, quality and commitment to provide African-American women with an experience of empowerment via her conference that literally changes their life in a positive and productive way.

So often women approach me and ask, "how do I get started with my dream, my goal, my passion?" There is no one successful map or stratagem. You simply have to get started right where you are. However, I can offer one answer by sharing Maria's thoughts since so many of you want to be self-employed.

In spite of her busy schedule of family, business and traveling, Maria has written her testimony of turning her passion into a profit. Here's her story....

MARIA DENISE DOWD

I am a staunch believer in destiny, or as my good friend Iyanla puts it, divine order. I believe we are all pre-disposed to serve a particular need on this earth. We all have a vocation and I believe the vocation is determined before our arrival on this planet. God provides the direction or calling. It is then up to us to listen and respond to that calling.

I listened and responded to my calling after quitting job number 22. I always knew I wanted to work for myself, and having grown up in a family of entrepreneurs, I wasn't the least bit intimidated by the prospect of flying solo.

I must admit that I wasn't quite sure what type of business I wanted to run, but inspiration struck in—of all places—the mall. I was under contract as a coordinator for Essence Magazine's "Essence on the Mall Show" and its "Cover Model Search" in 1989, when I realized I could offer African American women something they've been missing—a women's conference geared to their needs, their challenges and their dreams.

So, with a little bit of money and a lot of faith, I produced my first African American Women's Conference in my native San Diego in 1991. African American Women on Tour is now in its seventh year. I wish I could say that all of those years have been successful, but my passion hasn't been without personal and professional pitfalls.

I've learned over the years, however, that most businesses experience setbacks and dramas, but successful entrepreneurs are the ones who persevere despite seemingly insurmountable odds. Successful entrepreneurs are the ones who turn a deaf ear to naysayers.

I don't believe that I—as the slang goes—"got it going on" anymore than the next person. We all possess aptitudes— God given gifts—that begin to surface at a very early age. That gift may be artistic, oratorical, organizational, spiritual or intellectual.

My saving grace was to be blessed with a family that recognizes individual potential, and rarely tried to embarrass me into "settling down" or discourage me from pursuing my dreams.

I think it's important for us to recognize passion in our children and hone their God-given talents. A boy who spins humorous "wild stories" to save himself from some "hands-on-discipline" could be showing early signs of becoming a fiction writer. A girl who seems to be too obsessed too soon with her hair and your makeup could become a cosmetics giant.

Unfortunately, too many of our children are growing up in environments where their creative spirits are snuffed out by indifference or ignorance. Also, too many of our children don't have enough exposure to entrepreneurs who could serve as living proof that dreams do come true.

Much has been said about a village raising a child, but in the absence of these types of role models for all of our children, I believe it is the responsibility of the village to encourage children in youthful endeavors.

If you are fortunate, you and the people within your environment will support, invest, embrace and help you cultivate your passion. Remember, don't be discouraged. Just be quiet and listen, "your destiny is calling."

I am thankful to Maria Denise Dowd for her courage to listen and obey Spirit's direction for her life. Because of her God given talents, willingness to learn as she grew and commitment to excellence without excuse, thousands of women and young girls' lives have been transformed and informed.

The title of this book is dedicated to the memories and friendships made while working with my sisterfriend Maria, affectionately named by me, ***The Conference Diva*** and her awesome "crew" that work so hard to produce the nation's foremost Black women's empowerment conference.

The phone number for AAWT is in the appendix. Call toll free to receive a brochure and learn when the next conference is scheduled. You'll hear and experience nationally acclaimed keynote speakers, authors, business/career forums, spiritual and cultural renewal, village marketplace of art, jewelry, clothes, books, entertainment, rites of passage for girls, informative workshops, and networking. All egos are checked at the door. "Don't cheat yourself...treat yourself." If you are ready to recharge and take charge of your life, I'll see you there!

4

SISTERFRIENDS IN BUSINESS....
TAKE CARE OF BUSINESS

My father was a jewelry store owner, that's why I was given the name JEWEL. He was a gemologist and entrepreneur in Washington D.C. where I was born. Many other relatives in my family are self-employed. They say "the apple doesn't fall too far from the tree." So it was no far stretch of imagination for me to eventually be self-employed, as a motivational speaker. I've learned a lot of lessons on this journey which still continue today.

I enjoy reading a sisterfriend's fine publication entitled Minorities in Business published by Cynthia Butler-Hayden. She offers the following insights:

CYNTHIA BUTLER-HAYDEN

Obstacles are stepping stones. Throughout turbulent times, never lose your faith. You are blessed with support from friends and family. Like most people, we need support and encouragement. You have to constantly remind yourself that all your efforts will be worthwhile once you achieve your goals.

Armed with faith, determination and perseverance, anyone can achieve their goals. The power of the human mind is the most powerful force in the universe. As she thinks, so is she. What we conceive with integrity, hard work, education and a positive spirit, we can accomplish.

If you wish to take the leap of faith into the world of entrepreneurship, study the following tips and checklist to succeed and sustain your business.

Be creative and unique. Show up everywhere. Affirm that you are always in the right place at the right time. Be prepared for all challenges. Strive for quality, professionalism, competitive pricing and the best customer service. Your best advertisement is a satisfied customer. Master your field. Stay current with information, trends and changes. Follow through, complete what you start. Seek the professional assistance of those that can further advance your business, image and income. Be fair, honest and friendly. Integrity establishes longevity.

You are talented! Trust your abilities and your inner voice. Don't be your own worst enemy and critic. Conquer your fears and procrastination. Don't give up. Your main thing is to keep the Main Thing....THE MAIN THING.

Your CHECKLIST!

__ finances/budget/operating funds

__ business plan

__ goals/expectations/strategy

__ selling technique

__ manufacturing

__ distribution

__ warehousing/storage

__ advertising

__ networking

__ mentor

__ business literature

__ hiring/personnel

__ pricing

__ insurance

__ taxes

__ time management

__ work environment

__ operating equipment

__ special skills

__ self-esteem

__ internet

__ discipline

__ associations

___ education

___ attitude/personality

___ health habits

Do it well! Do it grand! Prosper my sister !

5

PROSPERITY MOTIVATION

Some people think of money in terms of survival and security only. Their fear-based limited thinking, procrastination, lack of knowledge, social conditioning, past family and personal experiences are blockages to their prosperity. You can only think, live, imagine, act and prosper as far as your knowledge will take you.

If self-knowledge and environment tells you that "it's lonely at the top," "I live from payday to payday," "Money is evil and not spiritual," "You don't have enough education," "You've had too many failures," "Find a safe, secure and sensible job," "Because you are a minority, wrong gender, wrong color, wrong neighborhood, wrong school, handicapped, on welfare, divorced, foster child, single parent....you'll never make it".

If you internalize these messages to be true....struggle and survival are your daily reality. Instead, you could be taking leaps of faith <u>and</u> action to experience more money, more life, more choices, more happiness and more financial freedom.

Poverty needs no plan, but PROSPERITY does! Your prosperity increases when your <u>knowledge</u> increases. Your <u>self-worth</u> increases when your <u>creative imagination</u> increases. Your <u>network</u> of people who are productive, achievers and mentors increases when your <u>integrity</u> increases. Your <u>faith</u> increases when your focused <u>actions</u> increase.

To put fresh water into a glass that is already full of water from yesterday, you will have to pour out the old stale water first.

It's the same way with your mind. It's difficult to put new information into your mind....until you empty it of the "money limiting" thoughts from yesterday. My desire is to help you "<u>un</u>learn" what keeps you financially limited before you "learn" new money increasing ideas.

To change your income, you want to change: (A) what you *think* about money (B) what you *think* about yourself (C) what you *do* to earn money.

You live *by unconscious rules and thoughts* <u>until</u> they are *consciously* changed. Your purpose for reading this material is to change your thoughts.

The conscious part of your mind feels, sees and hears money information from parents, school, TV, family, society, media, church and peers. The subconscious part of your mind believes the information is true. It doesn't judge what is in the "safe." This aspect of your mind becomes memories, perceptions, feelings and relationships with others.

The *conscious* part of your mind is the THINKER. The *subconscious* part of your mind is the PROVER. If the THINKER says "money is scarce, limited, only for the lucky, a struggle," the PROVER (based on memory and perception) will do everything to prove the THINKER is correct.

If the THINKER part of your mind says "money is abundant, you are worthy, you can pay your bills, you will find another job, you can travel, you can have a beautiful home," then the PROVER (based on memory and perception) does everything to prove the THINKER is correct.

The PROVER keeps the THINKER from going insane. It's duty and purpose is to look for people, information and circumstances that <u>confirm</u> what is in the subconscious mind. It wants to keep what the THINKER experiences in the outside world <u>consistent</u> with the stored information of the inside world. Have you heard the saying?

"If you think you CAN....you CAN. You're right.

If you think you CAN'T....you CAN'T. You're right."

The PROVER is the EGO. It wants to be right and is stubborn. Ego doesn't want to let go of fear. Ego doesn't want

41

to believe or receive new information. The ego guards the "safe."

E.G.O. = <u>E</u>asing <u>G</u>od <u>O</u>ut

I want to motivate you to invite God-thoughts into your mind. God-thoughts are <u>good</u>-thoughts about abundance, happiness, plenty, creativity, worthiness, prosperity and the ability to enjoy earning, spending, investing, saving and sharing money.

Before I share with you life changing, money increasing, mind-liberating thoughts about YOU and MONEY, first we need to reveal the common myths and mistaken ideas about money prosperity. This is how we "empty the glass" first of the *old stinkin' thinkin' thoughts*. Even a farmer knows he must pull up the weeds before he can plant new seeds.

Are you willing to know what the PROVER (your subconscious) has locked away in your mental "safe?" Your ego (prover) may resist because it has operated on old false information for so long. New wealth building ideas may not match the money-limiting beliefs locked away, secure and guarded by the PROVER. Trust me, the ego has to <u>go</u>, so good God-thoughts can come in.

Negative thought patterns perpetuate poverty and attitudes that repel, limit, confuse, discourage and deny you opportunities to save, earn, attract and enjoy abundance.

MONEY MYTHS

You have to work *hard* to earn money. If you enjoy what you do for a living, it is not real "work" and you can't make any money unless it is a hard, unpleasant struggle.

If you get the right education, the right school, the right family....you are guaranteed a great lifestyle, job and income.

To be happy and successful, you must please your parents, peers or mate.

Money is evil. If you acquire too much money, it is not spiritual.

Anyone who has a lot of money must be crooked, a criminal or a sinner. They probably earned it at the expense of others. Honest, good and caring people can't be prosperous.

It's lonely at the top. "If I improve my lifestyle, I may lose friends or never find someone to love me. Maybe I should remain in a struggle so I won't be alone."

My past (welfare, bankruptcy, repossessions, poor credit, unemployment, low income, family history, teen parent, poor grades in school, no college degree, divorced, minority, physical challenge, age, business failures, etc.) keep me from prosperity.... "I can't; they won't let me; it's impossible; I need affirmative action; it's too late for me." (These are victim beliefs that impoverish you.)

Parents, school and society teach you that you have to work hard to earn love. You're punished for being different and conditioned to play it safe and conform. Their fears, expectations and dominance limit and control your self-worth, creative thoughts and leaps of faith. False limitations are created and *you are now challenged to replace them.*

CHECK YOUR MONEY PERSONALITY

SPENDER....Credit Cards, impulsive gambler, shop 'til you drop, (instant gratification), shop to cure loneliness, boredom, depression.

SELFISH....What are your attitudes about the needs of your children, aging parents, friends, mate and yourself? Do your pleasures and desires come before family priorities or helping the less fortunate? Are you a miser? Are you overcautious or afraid to spend money?

SLEEPER....Are you in *denial* about your spending habits, retirement planning, improving your skills/education to boost your earning potential? Procrastination is a thief!

SPIRITUAL....Are your religious/spiritual dogmas, rituals, tithing, belief systems compatible with your mate? Do you believe/practice tithing? Do you believe God wants you to be poor? Do you believe in the spiritual laws of abundance?

SECRECY....What are your money practices in your

relationship? Do you have secret or separate banking/checking accounts? Do you discuss, plan and agree on major purchases? SHARING....Do you give too much? Do you help others with a hidden motive? Do you share information, resources or volunteer?

STUDIED....Do you *read* financial books on investments, loans and wealth building ideas?

FOUR WAYS TO INCREASE YOUR MONEY

(1) You WORK (physical labor, work for others, put in the long hours, paid according to your time not always your talent, education or worth).

(2) Your IDEAS WORK (inventions, business ideas, find a need and fill it, allow yourself to dream, your creative ideas can turn into dollars).

(3) OTHER PEOPLE WORK FOR YOU (Leaders know how to tap into the brainpower, manpower, talent and resources of others. If you develop good managerial and people skills, your money can increase while your physical labor decreases. Good leaders know how to find the right people to fulfill their dreams).

(4) YOUR MONEY WORKS FOR YOU (The most ideal way to increase wealth is mastering the laws of investments; real estate, wise business ventures, stocks, retirement plans, etc.).

THE FIVE LAWS OF MONEY

Scientific laws govern the universe. There are traffic and civil laws. There are laws that protect your body and spirit. There are school laws. There are spiritual laws and commandments. Parents have laws for their children's well-being. When laws and rules are ignored or misunderstood, chaos occurs. Laws and rules protect and maintain order.

There are money laws too! If you don't know these laws, you have no financial order or protection from life's emergencies and setbacks. If you know these laws and don't adhere to them, you have financial disorder. If you know these money laws and only obey the ones you like and ignore the rest, you never have consistent financial freedom.

To free yourself from financial distress, here are these five money laws:

(1) EARNING LAW: When you improve your skills, education and belief system about money, your income improves also. The more you learn….the more you can earn.

(2) SPENDING LAW: Change your thoughts about "spending" to "circulating" money. Understand that money multiplies and returns back to you. Circulate your money wisely knowing that each dollar goes through many transactions before it returns to you.

Each transaction produces a profit. Profit is the multiplication factor that operates on your expenses that *more* will return to you. Circulate cash and avoid the credit spending trap except for large purchases.

(3) SAVING LAW: There's an old Jamaican saying, *"Save money and it will save you."* Saving money is a learned habit. If you develop the habit of saving, you can respond to emergencies and opportunities.

The ideal rule is to save at least 10% of your income. Successful savers believe in paying themselves FIRST. Saving regularly is an affirmation in the abundance of money rather than lack.

(4) SPIRITUAL TITHE LAW: If you order and eat food from a restaurant and leave without paying for it, not only would you be rude, but you would be arrested for stealing food for your body.

When you receive spiritual blessings, comfort and grace

from the Lord, it is also likened to stealing, if you do not give back and support those responsible for your spiritual "faith food." Your church, prayer partner or any source that provides you and/or the less fortunate with spiritual support and insight are worthy of your tithes (10% of your income).

(5) INVESTING LAW: Investing is the spending of your capital with the purpose of earning a higher return than your savings can yield. Examples of investments are as follows: your own business, real estate, limited partnerships, securities, bonds, stocks, currency, second mortgages, art collections, rare coins, stamps, gems, precious metals or antique cars.

I am aware that I've discussed each of these laws with just a simple outline. If you are motivated and really want to pursue ways to increase your income, go to the library or your local bookstore to gain more in depth knowledge and practical applications.

You're the best person you could ever invest in. Empower yourself to believe that you are worthy and capable of a prosperous life. Get wealth building ideas! Have a mentor who is living the lifestyle and has the "money mindset" that you wish to achieve.

The future is where you will spend the rest of your life, so prepare for it. Discipline is <u>doing</u> what you have to do <u>NOW</u>, so you will be <u>free to do whatever you want to do later</u> in life. Become motivated to be a wealth builder based on *inspiration* rather than *desperation.*

Your beliefs and attitudes about money will change the more you read material like this book. Once your thinking and behavior change....your income will change too!

FOOD FOR THOUGHT FOR FINANCIAL HEALTH

Discard all superstitious beliefs. Do not ever regard money as evil or filthy. If you do, you cause it to take wings and fly away from you. Remember you "lose what you condemn."

Wealth is a conscious state. Feeling poor is a state of mind. Not having any money can be a temporary situation. Don't say you are "broke," instead say, "My money is circulating!" Write down your financial goals. "Poverty is a dis-ease. It is a dis-<u>fund</u>-tional lifestyle." There is a positive way to handle your financial concerns and challenges. (Suggestion: Don't use the word "problems")

Wealth is the ability to GIVE and RECEIVE. *It is your Father's good pleasure to give you the kingdom.* (Luke 12:32) Prayer is dynamic! Action is dynamic! Overcome negative thinking! ONE GOOD IDEA can create thousands of dollars!

SISTERFRIENDS

Imagine that others are happy, joyous, rich and provided for and rejoice in their prosperity and success. Never block someone else's opportunity to grow, advance or to prosper.

Have an attitude of gratitude. Think positive, speak your word for strength, courage, discipline, joy, wisdom and success.

Take time each day to be quiet, visualize the outcome you expect, give thanks and remind yourself of your worthiness. Re-commit to your goals and plans. Detach yourself from the world of stress, striving, worry, hurry, lack or limitation. Commune with the Spirit to be lifted up and receive blessed assurance that all your needs will be met.

Let your job be a joy! Be trustworthy, dependable and have integrity. People and circumstances are unpredictable.

Pray and seek guidance for prosperous ideas. Then follow through on your ideas. Write the letters "TYG" (Thank You God) on every check you write and every check you receive next to your signature endorsement. This affirms and reminds you of infinite abundance. Whenever you receive a bill for anything, immediately give thanks that you have received the same amount.

Plan, Prioritize, Pray, Be Positive, Persist and Prosper. "You know these things....now do them! If you can find happiness in the small things....if you can take care of and

50

master the small things….then you can be trusted to take care of larger things. Use your time and energy wisely.

Overcome procrastination. It is a thief! Finding your life's work satisfies your soul, and money will be the by product. Give your best. Do your best. Find a need and fill it. Don't allow people or circumstances to discourage, defeat or delay you. Overcome your greatest enemy….self-doubt. Never give up!

SELF-TALK MONEY AFFIRMATIONS

My work prospers me and others.

I am a money magnet.

People seek my services and products.

I am successful in all my endeavors.

I have an attitude of gratitude.

I am worthy of money and success.

I associate with prosperous
minded people.

I save money. I pay myself first.

My mind is open to receive.

I earn an excellent income that meets all my
financial needs and lifestyle.

I now establish order in my financial affairs.

I am willing to work and give
quality service and/or products.

My cup runneth over.
I gladly tithe and help others.

I am wealthy in ideas, health, relationships,
income and opportunities.

I train my mind for discipline, wisdom and faith in my
money thinking and habits.

I am too blessed to be stressed about money!
God is my Source!

You probably can identify with one of the following profiles and financial lifestyle. You are the patient and the doctor when it comes to your financial health. Are you financially sick or financially healthy?

No-Growth Profile	Success-Growth Profile
Too stressed to develop themselves.	Takes time to read, study and learn.
Overwhelmed with daily issues, too tired and can't see beyond present conditions.	Lives in comfort, wealth, mobility. Motivated to maintain wealth, lifestyle or motivated to rise above low income.
Seeks stress-release activities like TV, drinking, sleeping, drugs, shopping.	Seeks ways to make more money. Willing to work hard, read, plan. Idea oriented.
Associates with people who are also stuck, undereducated, oppressed, depressed, and unmotivated.	Associates with others on same or higher level of socio-economic level, seeker of mentors, new circles of people/info.
Too insecure to be around achievers or those who could increase their growth opportunities.	Takes advantage of networking, follows through on new contacts, referrals, new opportunities.
Spends money for instant gratification and basic survival needs. Reactive.	Invests money, saves money. Proactive.
Money habits learned from family, environment.	Money habits learned by family or consciously seeks other ways to increase income. Reads financial material.

I am certainly NO expert on financial matters. I have been up "fools hill" many times with foolish financial mistakes. I am a student seeking to become financially healthy. My desire is to present motivation and empowerment in every area of your life (relationships, health, self-esteem, faith, goals, business, parenting, cultural esteem, youth and money).

I remember hearing my sisterfriend, Iyanla Vanzant, author of Acts of Faith, Value in the Valley, and many more best-sellers. Iyanla was speaking at the African-American Women's Conference on Tour. Her point was that the three most important issues that Black women need to heal from are "men, mothering and money." I agree. We get hung up trying to control men, children, unexpected upsets in our life and most of us still haven't learned how to control and manage our money.

So sisterfriends, I have invited Glinda Bridgforth, a financial expert and author of The Basic Money Management Workbook to share her insights with all of us. Her services offer sisterfriends strategies to organize, record-keeping, develop spending plans, identify and understand their belief systems and emotional traits that subconsciously affect saving and spending patterns.

GLINDA F. BRIDGFORTH

"Nearly 50% of marriages today end in divorce and money is

the number one cause. Over 90% of today's women will make major financial decisions in life because they will become widowed, divorced or may choose to never marry. Nearly 75% of the elderly poor in this country are women."

These are shocking and frightening statistics. It's no wonder that many African American women today suffer from the "bag lady syndrome," a fear of one day ending up homeless and living out of shopping bags. It's enough to make a sister stay in bed and pull the covers over her head! As comforting as that thought may seem at times, we all know it's not the answer. So what can we do to avoid making the dreaded syndrome a reality in our lives?

First, we can begin to take personal responsibility of our finances or be personally involved with our family's finances whether or not we are the primary wage earner.

Secondly, we must take a holistic approach to cash flow and debt management by exploring the emotional, practical and spiritual aspects of our money relationship.

Most of us already know what we need to do to manage money more effectively. We know that we need to save more and spend less. But why is it that we don't do this consistently? Why can so many intelligent, well-educated, African American women successfully manage million dollar budgets for their employers and at the same time have their personal finances out of control? Exploring emotional aspects and belief systems can give great insight into why we often sabotage ourselves and the best laid financial plans.

Self Esteem

"Lee's father abandoned her family when she was eight months old. Her father, however, developed a close relationship with her older sister before he left, and each year lavished her with gifts while ignoring Lee. This emotional deprivation contributed to Lee's low self esteem and made her feel that she wasn't good enough. As an adult, Lee spent money on fancy dishes, kitchen appliances, clothes, etc. whenever she became angry or depressed. Once she even purchased a fur coat because her husband was out of town on their wedding anniversary."

The way we behave with money is a direct reflection of how we feel about ourselves. Many of us overspend to buy love, fill emotional voids, fend off rejection, anger, and depression. We think "retail therapy," will make us feel better. It does temporarily, but buyer's remorse sets in before we get home. We wonder how to pay for the items. Dealing with the cause of negative emotions is a critical first step. Addressing *it directly and resolving it instead of trying to alter the mood or fill the void by spending is a healthy behavior that will have long lasting positive benefits and curb financially destructive patterns.*

For women who chronically need to raise their self-esteem, or who feel there is never enough money, love, affection, attention, etc., Dr Brenda Wade, a San Francisco psychologist, suggest sitting quietly and affirming to yourself, I am enough. I have enough. I know enough. I do enough. Repetition is a powerful way to reprogram you subconscious to accept these ideas as reality.

Deprivation

"Theresa grew up in a single parent household. Her mother worked long hours and sometimes two jobs to support herself and her young daughter. Theresa's mother was extremely frugal in her spending and rigid as she saved what money she could. Theresa felt her childhood was one of lack, scarcity and deprivation. As an adult, Theresa spent....and spent....and spent. She eventually spent herself right into bankruptcy."

Most of us didn't have parents who sat us down at the kitchen table and taught us how to make a budget, balance a checkbook, or manage money. Most often, they didn't teach us because they themselves didn't know. However, we indirectly absorbed and internalized their attitudes, values, fears and frustrations about money. We then either emulated or rebelled 180 degrees against those values and behaviors.

Theresa consciously or subconsciously went to the opposite extreme from her mother's behavior. As an adult, no matter how much money she spent, clothes she bought or fun she had, it would never compensate or change her childhood deprivation. Coming to terms with that fact and acknowledging "money hurts" from her past was the beginning of healing for Theresa and her finances.

Make sure that you have balance in your monthly spending plan. If you are "anorexic" in one area of spending, you will probably "binge" in another. So be sure to allocate money for basic necessities, personal care, debt repayment, savings, and fun.

Fear

"Lenore was very proud of her accomplishment. A four bedroom, three bath house in the suburbs of Los Angeles that she shared with her two sons and her husband of 16 years. They had worked extremely hard to reach this level and sacrificed for years to make the house a reality. Lenore was never able to make this house her "dream home." Yes, the house was immaculate and so stylishly furnished that it could *easily make the cover of Architectural Digest. Yes, she and her husband were involved in the community and church. The kids participated in school and extra curricular activities.*

However, a nightmare lurked behind closed doors. Lenore suffered emotional, verbal and physical abuse that was far from a dream. Whenever asked why she stayed, her response was, 'What....and leave all of this'?"

There are many cases of domestic violence reported each year and there are many which are unreported. Often sisters are afraid to walk out of such circumstances for a variety of reasons. Sometimes fear of death threats made by their spouses or partners cause them to remain. Sometimes they are addicted to these toxic relationships and are afraid that if they leave, no one else will want them.

As in Lenore's case, they sometimes stay for image reasons. African American women often need to show visible success signs. It can be in the homes we own, the clothes we wear, the cars we drive, etc. Loss of status, lifestyle and financial benefits can become more important than safety, dignity and self esteem. If this situation is part of your reality, start taking care of yourself. Get support. Seek help from a professional therapist to assist you in making the emotional transition. Also find a financial counselor who can help create the plan for economic empowerment in your new life.

59

Money Messages and Myths

"Girls are not good at math. Girls are not good with money. They can't understand it. A man will come along and take care of you."

Nicole felt she was living the American Dream. A well-educated, successful career woman, wife, and mother of two children. She lived in the right neighborhood....her kids went to the right school...she drove the right car....and her family took the right vacations.

Nicole concentrated on building a career and taking care of her family with her husband of 12 years. He managed the family finances while she enjoyed a wonderful lifestyle.

All was great in her world until the day she received a telephone call from a creditor requesting payment. And then another call....and another. Before long it was apparent the extent of her husband's money mismanagement. Ultimately, Nicole found her family's assets had been completely liquidated and they were nearly bankrupt.

What were the money messages you heard as a child and how have they affected your adult belief systems? Did you buy into the myth as Nicole did, that women are incapable of managing money and that we should turn over complete control of our finances to men? Or are you waiting for Mr. Right to come along before you get your financial life in order?

Women are just as capable as men of successfully managing money. Because we have the ability to admit a lack of knowledge and seek information or support when needed, this makes us more capable.

African American women must do three things in accepting personal responsibility for our finances:

Homework—*Set goals and target dates. Pick goals that really motivate you and create burning desires. For example: a new home, a Caribbean vacation or an investment portfolio.*

Legwork—*Do the monthly basics. Balance your checkbook, create a spending plan or budget, track, add up and analyze your spending, pay off debts, and save regularly.*

Innerwork—*Develop spiritual practices. Pray and meditate daily. Go within, quiet your mind, connect with The Source of your good. Use affirmations which reprogram your subconscious mind to a positive consciousness. Practice visualizing success and prosperity. See your life with all of your wants and needs met.*

When we commit to these practices we gain control, maintain consistency in our healthy money habits and continue along the path to financial freedom.

6

SISTERFRIEND:
GET STARTED ON YOUR GOALS

Realization of a goal is less likely to manifest if the goal is lacking in detail, dates and a determined attitude. When you go to a restaurant, you can't just say, "I'm hungry." The waitress will ask you <u>what</u> do you want and <u>how</u> do you want it? When you go to the airport, you can't just say, "I need a vacation." The reservationist will ask you <u>where</u> do you want to go, <u>when</u> do you want to leave and when do you want to return? The waitress and reservationist are trained in customer service. They can better serve you when YOU KNOW what you want.

God's law of manifestation is the same. Spirit has the best "customer service department." What do you want? When clear thinking is <u>energized</u> with action and faith, people, conditions and opportunities are <u>magnetized</u> to you. That's why you're often warned, "Be careful what you ask for because you just might get it." Just like your food ordered in a restaurant and an airplane ticket have a cost attached, so does your dream. Are you willing to pay the cost of discipline, time, money, courage, commitment, endurance, service and giving to others.

Using words like "some day," "one day," "I wish," are weak and lack energy, conviction and faith. If your words and faith are vague, weak and fuzzy, you remain unfulfilled and frustrated. If your words, faith and actions are clear, dynamic, specific, focused and bold, you've tapped into the universal, unlimited and infinite supply of God. God is your SOURCE, but people are the reSOURCES.

NO DEPOSIT....NO RETURN

All your efforts are your deposit in God's universal bank. In return, you will be blessed, rewarded, empowered and delivered from setbacks. Opportunities that appear and positive conditions may seem like coincidences. I like the saying, "A coincidence is God's way of remaining anonymous." It's no coincidence. Your faith, words and works are being rewarded.

Spiritual laws are set into motion that respond to your giving, willing and obedient nature. Just try and go to a bank and ask for money. If there's no active account in your name, they look at you like you're crazy. They don't know you. They don't recognize you. They don't serve you. "No deposit....no return."

If man's bank operates that way, you can imagine the same policy in "The Universal Bank of the Most High."

CLEAR AND MEASURABLE GOALS

People and conditions will respond to fulfill your request. But if you feel unworthy, doubtful and unclear, you are blocking the flow of abundance to you. Speak up, place your order, become specific with dates, colors, prices, people, conditions, amounts, etc. Don't be afraid to say or ask for what you <u>really</u> want. Let this be your guide in helping you to make <u>measurable</u> and <u>clear</u> goals.

<u>Unclear</u>	<u>Clear</u>
I need more money.	I'm asking for a 15% increase in my salary. I will arrange for a meeting with my supervisor by the end of this week.
I need more fun in my life. Someday I'll take a vacation.	I'm going on a cruise to Jamaica <u>this</u> summer. Saturday I will go to the travel agency to get a brochure.
I need less stress in my life.	I'm going to create a more fulfilling job/career/business closer to home. The commute will be no more than____.

Unclear	**Clear**
I wish I had more energy.	Starting (date) I'm going to stop eating red meat, drink more water and workout each morning to my Aerobics with Soul video.
I'm tired of riding the bus. Someday I will get a new car.	This weekend I'm going to look at cars. I'm going to overcome my fear of prices, credit history and intimidation from sales people. Starting with my next paycheck, I will save $____ each time for my down payment. I will clean out my garage and prepare to enjoy and drive my new car (year, model, color) by (date).
When the children grow up, then I'll go back to my creative writing.	I will keep my talent fresh. I will continually write in my journal. I take time at least ____ hours a week to write. I will find a writer's class or support group to join by the end of THIS year.
One day I want to meet more people.	I will become active in networking, or participate in any positive, productive organziation where I can be around like-minded, active people. I will create time in

Unclear	Clear
	my schedule now to be active and open to growth in my social, personal, professional and spiritual life.
One day, when everything is guaranteed that I won't fail, I'll start my own business.	Catering and organizational skills come naturally for me. I will begin developing my marketing plan, customer referrals and some beginner business cards and brochures to test the market. I can do at least one or two events a month part-time, to supplement my income and determine if I really have the desire, talent and entrepreneurial qualities.
I wish I had more self-esteem.	The next time he raises his voice at me, I will respond to defend myself and let him know I'm no longer passive, intimidated or feeling unworthy. I will read, pray and study personal development and spiritual material that remind me of who I am. "I am worthy of love, peace of mind and respect everyday and in every way."

Unclear	**Clear**
I'm feeling insecure and bored about my job. Sometime soon I'll go back to school.	I will register for_____ class, finish it and become more active in upgrading my education and skills.
I'm going to start saving and/ or tithing more.	With my next check I will dedicate $____ each time to my savings and $____ to my spiritual source.
One day my relationship is going to get better. I'm praying that he'll pay more attention to me and make my life more exciting.	I will tell my mate that this weekend I have cleared my calendar and arranged for a babysitter. I will let him know how much I still enjoy being with him and that I want to go to dinner at the (restaurant) and to that new jazz club. I am willing to be more clear in sharing my feelings instead of waiting, assuming or brooding.

THIS SISTER ACTED ON HER GOALS...

The following letter stands out among the many letters received regarding feedback and results from attending my workshops at the African American Women on Tour Conference. I now share from a sisterfriend who attended one of my sessions from this awesome conference....

Dear Jewel,

I attended my first African-American Women's Conference on Tour (AAWOT) in Washington D.C. in 1994 and signed up for your workshop, "Stop Sitting on Your Assets." I said to myself, "I've never heard of Jewel Diamond Taylor, but the title of her workshop sounds motivating."

It got me to think about myself, and how I have been blessed with so many wonderful things in my life. Unfortunately, I was not using my creative talents to start my own business, change jobs or change my life.

Well, when I attended the AAWOT conference in 1995 in Atlanta, I had already started my travel business. I had my fliers (purple) done and sent them to AAWOT to enclose with the registration packets for all the AAWOT attendees. I was ready to get this travel business going.

Purple, as I remember you said, represented royalty. Also, I lost 35 pounds just by keeping your motivational words in my mind. My travel business is doing well and I now have two separate companies.

I remember your words: "Procrastination is the greatest 'wait loss' program in the world. The more you procrastinate and wait, the more you lose."

You asked, "What books are you not reading, what classes are you missing and am I using my time wisely? Set your priorities and act upon them."

"Don't spend major time with minor people."

"Stop sitting on your assets."

"Keep the main thing....THE MAIN THING."

Another point I took to heart was relationships with men. Since my mate was not on the same page with me, I had to let him go. I am worthy and should not give my time and energy to someone who doesn't see the good in me."

Jewel, I thank you very much. I am happy to have met you in 1994. You will always see me in your workshops at AAWOT. In fact, I'll be in three cities this year. I will have a travel booth set up.

May God bless you and your sister Joy, my sisterfriends. I would like to see you about buying your books to give to my business clients as incentives.

Sincerely,

Cynthia Brown

Global Destinations/New York.

Cynthia got busy on her goals. She acted on the information. I was just instrumental in reminding her of what she had forgotten.

You will eventually act on your goals from either desperation or inspiration. Women too often are reactive vs. proactive in their goalsetting. We tend to be more "now-oriented" than future-oriented. Thinking and acting on your future is proactive behavior that reaps results. If you wait until you are in a crisis, laid off, sick, tired, tempted, lonely, and broke....you make poor choices. Desperate times bring about desperate choices. Why not choose to be inspired by what you are learning to stop sitting on your assets....and get started on your goals!

What Are You Waiting For?
by Jewel Diamond Taylor

You've got books on the shelf to be read
words of kindness and apologies to be said
clothes in the closet still not worn
dreams on hold....waiting to be born
phone calls to make
memories and pictures to take
vacations delayed
decisions to be made
bills to be paid
       what are you waiting for?

there are resumes to write
classes you can take day or night
procrastination is a thief
you've got opportunities to seize
bad habits to decrease, and better habits to increase
kisses, hugs and smiles to give and receive
God's peace and promises to believe
       what are you waiting for?

there are things that need fixin' and cleaning
and a life that needs meaning
your goals you need to think and ink

there are those who need your love and time
your money needs to be saved and tithed
you've got overdue prayers for the Lord
       'cause you've so much to be thankful for

there's paperwork and projects to complete
you've got places to go and people to see
your ideas need focus and action
and there's questions you need to be askin'
       what are you waiting for?

Your body needs healthy foods & exercise to feel alive
tender loving, quiet time for your spirit and mind.
You need relationships that are nurturing and kind

Ice is melting, leaves are falling, clocks are ticking,
       death is whispering in your ear....
"Do it now....enjoy life....
       what are you waiting for?"

7

TOO BLESSED TO BE STRESSED

I clearly remember coming home from a Houston speaking engagement in 1994. My younger sister, Joy Lewis-Anderson, works and travels with me as my promoter. She markets my motivational products and coordinates membership/events for my national motivational support network, The Enlightened Circle.

We were returning from a very successful and enjoyable business trip. My husband greeted us at the airport and the three of us stood talking and waiting for our luggage. It soon became evident that my luggage did not make the trip with me. All of a sudden I had an attitude. "Oh, no they didn't," I said with the neck action going. "How could they do this?....I have some of my favorite outfits and shoes in that luggage....my jewelry....they better find it!!"

I paced the floor. Questioned the "tired - I could care less - this happens all the time - what's the big deal" luggage claims airport attendant." I walked back again to the ramp hoping my delinquent cherished belongings would appear. My sister had all her luggage. We travelled together, so where was mine? Don't they know who I AM?

Sisters....I was stuck on stupid. And then all of a sudden a small voice within said, "What are you so upset about? Whatever was in that luggage can be replaced. You get to travel and work with your sister. You both had an enjoyable and profitable time. You sold all your books. You made some money that is still in your purse. There were no emergencies while you were gone. Your family is safe. The plane didn't crash. You need an "attitude of gratitude" because you are too blessed to be stressed!"

That small voice that we call God was right. I needed to check myself before I wrecked myself. My reality check told me that I had begun to take all the frequent flyer miles of safe travel for granted. I was still alive. My family is well. I can replace those items. There were many times in the growing stages of my career that I returned home with little profit. However, I was rich in more ways than one. This was an opportunity to be reminded of blessings and miracles that happen every day.

We have been pampered, spoiled and always in a hurry living in a world of instant gratification. Overnight or same day delivery, drive-thru fast food, pizza delivered to your home, microwave meals, faxes, call waiting, super information highway, cellular phones, and high technology. All these modern conveniences lower our tolerance.

Beware! It's a setup for a breakdown. You and I have become conditioned and expected to adapt to fast track living. So whenever there is a glitch, a human error or a waiting period, we have the *nerve* to get upset. The operative word is "nerve." Our *nervous* system is fragile and unforgiving. We allow people and conditions to dictate our state of mind. The mind and the body are connected.

If we allow people and external conditions to dictate our state of mind, we are giving our power away. The emotional state of the *mind triggers the body* to respond in many ways. When the mind is in turmoil, despair and stress, the results are many. Health problems, car accidents, destroyed relationships, depression, addictions, financial ruin and a multitude of other problems are unhappy lessons.

Ego and lack of faith can certainly be a hindrance to your peace of mind too. Therefore, personal development efforts and seeking spiritual guidance can better prepare you to cope with the unexpected, unfair and unwanted.

Learn how to LET GO of attitudes, habits, people or conditions that are harmful. If you're trying to DO too much,

BE too much, HAVE too much or WORK too much without time for family, leisure and meditation, you eventually pay a heavy price.

There are people and conditions you cannot change or control. If you can't cope in a healthy, peaceful, productive and peaceful manner to grief, setbacks, pain, fear or worries, then stress will occur in subtle or overt ways. The source can be confronted or ignored. You can choose to be reactive and always in a state of emergency or you can become proactive and live in a state of grace.

Sisters, we suffer more than we should because somehow we feel if we could just only fix, rescue, manipulate, pray enough, control, love more, look better, work harder, sacrifice and struggle just a little more….it would be enough to turn conditions or someone around. There are many lessons in life to learn that can empower and set you free. If you no longer want to continue to create, promote or allow stress in your life….think about and act on these insights:

- You can't control how people think or act.

- You can't always protect your loved ones from pain.

- Love may disappoint and hurt, don't let it destroy you….love again.

- You may not always feel appreciated or understood, so keep your self-esteem and self-worth in tact.

- Let go of people, habits or conditions that are harmful, negative or unworthy of your time.

- People and circumstances are <u>un</u>predictable, so be prepared and don't assume anything.

- You <u>can't</u> do everything for everybody....decide which things need to be <u>done</u>....<u>delegate</u> or <u>dump</u> the rest.

- Follow through on what you start.

- Practice better time management....be on time.

- Find pleasure and gratitude in the small things in life.

- Life is too short to hold onto dead issues....let them go.

- Let go of grudges, it's stealing your joy.

- Being angry, selfish, unreliable, dishonest, rude, worried and always in a hurry blocks your blessings. Be honest about your character flaws and work on them.

- Have cleanliness and order in your home and workplace, it keeps you organized and less frustrated.

- When stress appears, stay away from the wrong coping behavior of drinking, eating, fighting, sleeping or shopping....learn positive coping behavior. Exercise, go for a walk, fast, drink lots of water, enjoy nature, take deep breathes....it helps to create clear thinking.

• People are more important than things, discover ways to let your loved ones know that you care about them.

• Be observant of your surroundings, workplace and community—communicate vs. isolate—to avoid any sudden changes that could negatively impact your lifestyle.

• God is TOO Big to have *little* faith. If you are having financial, health, love or career challenges, trust God to move in mysterious, mighty and miraculous ways. If worried, why pray? If you pray, why worry!?!?!?

Several years ago I wrote seven short prayers so I could read them and be lifted up while at work, in the car or while standing in line at the bank. There are usually seven areas in our lives that concern us. And sometimes we are so overwhelmed with worry, stress or grief that words don't come easily. I gladly share my "Seven Pearls of Prayer" with you so you can affirm and focus on the positive.

Even though the words may not reflect what is happening right now in your life, praying affirmatively speaks it into existence and changes your mind. The words and feelings change your mind to become peaceful and receptive. FAITH (affirmative prayer) focuses on what you do want, while FEAR focuses on what you don't want.

Your consciousness, conversation and conditions change when you change your focus. Whatever you give attention to....increases. Where attention goes, energy flows. The *intention* of affirmative prayer directs your *attention* away from stress and *towards* Spirit filled solutions. God's energy is abundant, sacred, divine and *unlimited.* There are more than one or two answers to your dilemma. Don't limit yourself by talking about, thinking about, complaining and projecting what you don't want to happen or what you think will happen. Stress limits God's ability to flow through you in the manifestation of answers, peace, guidance and blessed assurance. In other words, you are *too stressed to be blessed.*

Stress and challenges in your life are an invitation to grow. An opportunity to evolve to a higher way of thinking. (going to the "Upper Room")

The "Seven Pearls of Prayer" is something you can read daily or be creative and write your own.

SEVEN PEARLS OF PRAYER

(1) FOR MY FINANCES....My wealth comes from expected and unexpected sources. I have more than enough money coming in and going out. I am a responsible and wise money manager. I work, save, tithe and invest to keep money circulating to me and others. All my financial needs are met and I pay all my debts because I know that God is MY source. I am led and fed by the Spirit. I am too blessed to be stressed.

(2) TO MY LOVED ONES....You are surrounded by God's presence, protection and supply. I release any anxiety about your well-being. I will not blame, criticize or condemn. Your way may not be my way, but I trust the Spirit of God in you to show you the way to your highest good. I let go of ego, pride, worry, struggle and control. I am learning that everyone in my life is a teacher and in my life for a reason or a season. I send peace, blessings and love your way....every day!

(3) FOR MY ATTITUDE....I choose my thoughts with care. I am in the process of positive change. I keep my thoughts focused on good. I am grateful for all my blessings and opportunities. My life is getting better and better every day. I am excited about being in control of my life and making better decisions. Today is a great day. I will make it so. Everything is in divine order.

(4) LETTING GO OF WORRY....God is within me and around me. Doubt shuts out the light and love of God. I am easily and divinely guided to solve my challenges. I am led and fed by the Spirit. Worry only changes me physically and emotionally, it does not change any circumstances. I am developing faith, self-esteem, courage and a proactive lifestyle.

(5) FOR MY HEALTH...I see my body healthy, active and beautiful. Wellness is my priority. Everyday I am drinking more water, exercising, and eating fruits and vegetables which reduces stress in my life. I treat my body with respect, pampering, loving and healthy relationships that honor me physically, emotionally, mentally and spiritually.

(6) FOR MY RELATIONSHIPS....I am a loving and forgiving person. I attract loving and supportive relationships. I experience love, harmony and joy wherever I go. Like-minded people who share similar values, interests and a positive outlook on life are in my life. My self-esteem is healthy whether I am in an intimate relationship or not. I am worthy of the best.

I am worthy of wonderful personal and professional relationships. I radiate self-esteem, well-being, health and wholeness. I am a loveable person.

(7) FOR MY CAREER....My skills, talents and actions create the right career for me. I was created to be successful. My service creates value and a great income to meet my financial needs and creative skills. I work with and for wonderful people who appreciate my contributions. My ability to create more income is unlimited.

I maintain balance in my life with family, leisure and career. I stay informed and proactive in the workplace. I am organized and a dependable asset to my team. I keep my career goals and skills current. I do not take rejection or disappointments personally. When one door closes, another will open because I am proactive, professional and have faith.

During troubled times, you can have blessed assurance, perfect peace and strong faith. If you can feel and really understand the words of Psalms 23, then you will know why I say "I'm too blessed to be stressed."

The Lord is my Shepherd (perfect salvation)

I shall not want (perfect satisfaction)

He maketh me to lie down in green pastures (perfect rest)

He leadeth me beside still waters (perfect refreshment)

He restoreth my soul (perfect renewal)

He leadeth me in the paths of righteousness (perfect guidance)

I will fear no evil (perfect protection)

Thou art with me (perfect company)

Thy rod and Thy staff (perfect comfort)

Thou preparest a table (perfect provision)

Thou annointest my head (perfect consecration)

My cup runneth over (perfect joy)

Surely, surely (perfect confidence)

Goodness and mercy shall follow me (perfect care)

I will dwell in the House of the Lord forever (perfect destiny)

You may not be perfect, your situation may not be perfect, life is not perfect, but isn't it comforting to know God's promises, protection and provisions are perfect.

This is the gospel (good news)....makes you wanna shout!

HOW TO STOP WORRYING

Staying busy is the cheapest medicine for worry. The more leisure time you have, the more time you have to be miserable and focus on what makes you so unhappy. Good, fruitful, rewarding work DOES NOT make you tired. Being bored, worried and self-absorbed makes you tired. Get busy being proactive. Move through the fear. Get interested in helping other people. Find your talents, hobbies and projects. Explore your personal growth.

Choose to profit from your mistakes or misfortunes. What can you learn? How can it be avoided in the future? Can you help someone else going through the same experience? Count your blessings. It could be worse. You are too blessed to be stressed! Stay prayed up. When the prayers go up, the blessings come down.

You can choose to be <u>concerned</u> and take action about conditions in your life or you can choose to <u>worry</u> and become paralyzed with fear.

Worry doesn't change anything but your blood pressure. Worrying affects your health. Both worry and stress silently kill your mental, physical, emotional, financial and spiritual well-being.

"The Lord may forgive us of our sins" said William James, "but the nervous system never does."

THINK ABOUT IT

This is a brand new day. You are blessed. Cancel your pity party. Can you still laugh, walk, talk, see, smell, touch?

Haven't you been shown grace, mercy, and forgiveness for past transgressions? Haven't you gotten a job before, had a new start? You can do it again! Can you teach, help, mentor, supervise, coordinate, lead, serve or motivate others? Are you "sitting on your assets?"

If you need something, have you asked....do you network....ask for referrals....look through your phone book....do you speak another language....do you have more than one skill or talent....are you using your time and money wisely....are you overlooking opportunities or people right where you live....have you read the books you already have....have you gone to the library....is there paperwork to be completed....phone calls to be returned....are you sleeping too much...is your resume current....how many people do you know....what classes or seminars are you missing....do you procrastinate....who has offered to help you....are you aware of the God-power within you to guide you....do you trust your intuition....have you forgotten how far you have come and what you have endured and what you have accomplished....are you still sitting on your assets?

Guilt, grief and pain are concerned with the past. Worry and stress are concerned with the future. Contentment, gratitude and peace are found only in the present.

8

IF YOU ENDURE AND PASS YOUR TEST....YOU WILL HAVE A TESTIMONY

As the elder wise ones tell us, "If you haven't been through some pain, the fire or a test of your faith yet....just keep on living."

Will you come out of your pain bitter, weakened and destined to repeat some lessons, or will life's trials and tests make you stronger, wiser and victorious?

I've had my share just like everyone. As a sisterfriend, speaker, spiritualist, student and counselor, I have heard some incredible testimonies of faith and endurance. I've also received countless letters, calls and prayer requests. Women have loved and lost, succeeded against odds, overcome addictions and painful chilhoods, redesigned their lives and contradicted society naysayers and family which said it couldn't be done.

Their stories of courage and determination are learning lessons. Now hear from a sisterfriend named Marcie Eanes.

DEAR SISTERFRIEND

All my help comes from God. It's a simple statement which took me over ten years to acknowledge and admit to others. My thinking was forever altered by various trials I've endured over this period. Only God brought me through them without bitterness and far greater joy than ever before.

My transformation began in 1985. I nearly died from injuries sustained in a car accident. When I awoke from a 10 day coma, I was paralyzed from the neck down. However, I had few difficulties thinking and speaking clearly.

It was a shock to go from independence to total dependence. I was only 23 and my future was very bright to all who knew me. I had just graduated from college and was employed as a newspaper reporter for The Grand Rapids Press in Grand Rapids, Michigan.

This was my dream job. My undergraduate career was filled with honors and internships with various publications. Graduation was icing on the cake. I didn't hesitate leaving family and friends in my home town of Racine, Wisconsin to move to a city where I knew no one. I saw it as the beginning of a great adventure.

I wasn't disappointed. The daily challenges of going to events and writing about them was an exhilarating one. My work day was unpredictable. Some days I worked eight hours, others stretched into 12-16 hours. None of this bothered me. I would've worked for free.

Although I had little social life, I managed to become friendly with many of my work colleagues. All was well until that fateful August night.

The impact of the two cars crashing together caused me to suffer severe whiplash. My neck was fractured in three places and my spinal column was nicked by bone shards. Doctors were uncertain how much mobility I would regain once I awoke from the coma. They agreed that I was extremely fortunate to have survived at all.

However I didn't feel lucky. All I could think and ask was, "why me?" It felt as if all the work I have done up to this point was a waste of time. I wished I would have died instantly.

My family and friends soon grew tired of my self pity. They helped me muster the strength to endure the many months of therapy which lay ahead of me. In time, I was able to walk with the aid of a cane. I also regained many motor skills I thought the accident took from me.

My body wasn't the only part of me which grew stronger. My faith in God was strengthened through prayer and meditation. Although my parents raised my brothers and me in a spirit filled home and sent us to religious based schools, I never felt a personal connection with Him. The accident forced *me to choose between becoming victimized by negative thinking or finding ways to lift myself out of despair. After a couple of years, I felt everything was finally settling down. I looked to the future with renewed hope.*

Little did I know God was preparing me for bigger challenges. Both my parents died by the time I was 28. My father, Bennie, 45, died suddenly of pneumonia in 1987. My mother, Dorothy, 51, died of stroke complications in 1990.

Once again I felt as if the rug had been pulled from under me. My parents were the center of my life. I was furious that the family I knew was no longer. Few understood my unspeakable grief.

Another component of this trying time was the care of my youngest brother, Christopher. He couldn't speak and had the mental capacity of a young child. He could do little by himself. My parents often said they didn't want Chris to become a burden for my two other brothers or myself. Unfortunately, they made no provisions for his care.

This task was left to my two brothers and myself. Initially, all of us cared for Chris. When my brothers got married and began lives with their spouses, nearly all the responsibility landed on my shoulders.

I felt trapped. Both brothers moved forward in their lives. I was the eldest, and nearly everything in my environment tethered me to the past. Chris and I shared the family home. Almost everything looked the same as when both my parents were alive. Nearly every nook and cranny of that four bedroom home held several memories. It soon felt like I was maintaining a shrine.

Adding to my emotional drain, was facing the fact I could no longer care for Chris. His health began rapidly deteriorating after Mom's death. By 1994, Chris needed more extensive help.

My faith in God was the only thing which helped me cope with these pressures. Shortly after Mom's death, I read Psalm 27. In it I found answers and comfort and soon it became an invitation to walk by faith, not by sight. I knew I needed to change my life, but lacked the courage to do it.

As I cried out to God one day, a soft voice told me to volunteer myself. At first I brushed it aside. I toyed with the idea when I graduated from college, but chose to pursue a job. I thought volunteer work was reserved for retired people and never thought I could do it after my accident. I thought no one would want me.

I was happy to be proven wrong. The Providence Volunteer Ministry Program selected me to become a second grade teacher's aide at a Catholic grade school in Hawthorne, California in 1994. I had roughly six weeks to get my affairs in order and move out of Wisconsin before school began in August.

91

My brothers were shocked at the news. They felt as if I was abandoning them. My plans further strained our already weak relationship. Little I said or did could help them accept the sale of the house and my decision to place Chris in the foster care system to receive the personal care I could no longer provide.

Although I was hurt by their reaction, I stuck to my plans. Again my friends stood by me. So did God. After a whirlwind month of selling everything, packing my bags and saying good-bye, I was on my way to my volunteer post. Nearly everyone fretted about my choice to move once again to a city with no immediate family and few friends. Their fears were calmed when I told them I would be living in a convent with eight sisters and another parish volunteer.

I loved my job. My volunteer year was more rewarding than I imagined it would be. The children taught me lifelong lessons about honesty, frankness and caring for others. Through my work as a grief counselor for fourth and fifth graders, I faced my own grief. I was also active within the church community and made many new friends. All of this was the catalyst I needed for my next big step.

When my volunteer year ended, I chose to remain in the area. I moved out of the convent and into a studio apartment. I expanded by social boundaries as well as returned to my *passion, writing. These changes broke me from the chains of my past at last.*

The trials haven't ended. My brother, Chris, died in 1996. I blamed myself for his death, but, once again, my friends wouldn't let my grief get the better of me. I now realize I did the best I could for Chris during those six years I was his caregiver. I'm honored God chose me. The lessons I've learned will never be forgotten.

I am still hopeful my two surviving brothers and I will make peace some day. Life's too short to keep the circle of blame going. We all made choices which proved to be the best for us as individuals. Only God knows when this reconciliation will happen.

All I can do is keep moving forward in my own life. Nearly all who know me say I seem more at peace than ever before. I laugh and smile more easily now. The challenge of another day doesn't frighten me anymore. My days are full of love, friendship and fun.

I've discovered another facet of myself after Chris' death. I began writing poetry. The discovery of this hidden talent led me to become involved in a writer's group which performs "live" at various venues around the Los Angeles area. I feel no inhibitions with my "up front and personal" performance style. I never tried writing poetry before, but now I can't stop.

Yes the last ten years have seen me shed many tears, but I now realize all those experiences made me into a new person. I know for certain I can do anything with God's help. As long as I let Him lead, all good things will come my way in due time. I can't wait to see what happens next.

Our communities are filled with sisters living with AIDS, diabetes, lupus, sickle cell anemia and cancer. These illnesses bring unique challenges that must be endured. They can affect self-esteem, finances, lifestyle, energy level, relationships, career and emotional well-being. We are charged and challenged to understand the plight of these individuals who feel invisible, undeserved, overwhelmed and alone. One sister I met has written a book to tell her story of living with another disease.

ARLINE DEAN HAS A TESTIMONY

Sharing with my sisterfriends is important. We all have different issues to live with and learn to cope with. I have one particular health issue that has caused me to reach out and share now. You see, I have Multiple Sclerosis and maybe some of you may be afflicted as well.

Since the onset of this disease, I have been forced to deal with many unexpected issues. Maintaining my self-esteem is one challenge. I had become self-conscious because of the way I walk. I withdrew and changed my lifestyle. Now, I'm learning and improving my self-esteem every day.

My courage has grown after doing several radio interviews, public speaking and booksignings. My book Multiple Sclerosis, The Unseen Enemy *has touched many lives. Because I am a Black woman, most of the questions I get are from Black women. Along with asking how I cope, I am frequently asked whether MS is more prevalent in the Black community. Finding support groups is another concern. I address these and other questions in my book. Until a cure is found, I plan to continue researching and being an activist for "MS." I now know in spite of all that has happened, I need to love and accept myself. I found the greatest love of all is inside of me.*

9

How to Avoid Burnout

Burnout happens when you ask too much of yourself. Burnout robs you of peace of mind, productivity and most all affects your health. Burnout happens to single parents working two jobs and have to act as both parents. It can happen if you're working all day and taking classes at night to further your education. Burnout can happen when you're working full-time for someone else and working your own business part-time.

Or maybe you're raising your grandchildren, taking care of an older sick parent or a physically challenged family member. If you are an overachiever, workaholic and martyr, your burnout is self-imposed because you take on too much responsibility or too many goals.

If you're ready to experience more peak performance, peace of mind and effective results in your life, consider the following points to stop feeling so burned up and spent up

SISTERFRIENDS

emotionally, physically, financially and spiritually. Stop, breathe, read, listen, listen, listen....

(1) Don't engage in blame, guilt and self-condemnation. Only give, serve or act from a state of love and peace. Don't continue taking on more responsibility, if you're not really sincere, ready, available, capable or willing....Okay?

(2) Simplify each day. Some things you must *delegate,* some things you'll have to *dump,* and some things have to get done....so *do it.* It's easier to accomplish this when your goals are *written down* in order of their priority. What's the *three* most important tasks at hand today? Focus on that first.

(3) If you don't slow down, you're more prone to make mistakes, accidents occur, conflict at home or work occurs and important details are overlooked. Don't move so fast....slow down....OKAY?

(4) Stop caring who gets the credit. Pride and ego keep you from growing and promotes isolation and alienation. Sisterfriend, allow others to help you. Be open to TEAMWORK. That's one positive working principle we can learn from men. Some tasks need to be performed by only you, but be open to accomplishing more with team work.

(5) Re-think your motives. *Why* are you doing what you are doing? *Who* are you doing it for? Is it that important? Is it in harmony with your *values* and goals? Will your actions *right now* get you closer to your immediate goal? Sometimes we live and act from other people's agendas, needs, demands, pressures and value system.

(6) Success is in the journey, not the destination. Are you enjoying the process or frustrated waiting for the finish? Striving for perfection creates stress and frustration. Hurry and worry creates unnecessary stress. Focus only on progress. Don't overlook the lessons on the way to your goal.

Whether you are waiting for your baby to be born, the college classes to end, writing a book, planning your wedding, starting your new business or remodeling your home....enjoy and relax. Practice being in the moment. This practice promotes well-being, attitude of gratitude and puts you in a state of grace. Look around and really notice where you are and how far you have come. "Smell the roses along the way."

(7) Are you trusting God to look after you, provide and work it out? Trust God more. I have a small plaque in my kitchen to remind me of letting go. It simply reads, "Before you go to bed....give your troubles to God. He stays up all night anyway."

(8) Don't be so hard on yourself. Lighten up. Develop a sense of humor. Take time for your family, leisure and meditation. If you love to paint, sing, dance, sew, write poetry, jog, fish, play cards, work in the garden, knit....do it....that's good therapy for the soul and keeps you sane. You shouldn't have to sneak in your fun time during lunch hour at work or when the family is gone or wait until you're on vacation. To be healthy and successful requires balance in your life. Neither working too hard or playing too hard is healthy or productive.

(9) Draw emotional boundaries. Don't be afraid to say "NO" to requests or demands that take you away from your peace of mind or progress towards your goal. If you know when to draw the line to people, conversations, disruptions, negative environments, temptations and distractions that steal your joy and opportunities in life....you are empowered. Here's my affirmation you can share with people who try to abuse your time, energy, peace and talent.

Don't confuse me with someone who is unfocused, lacking determination or weak in self-worth or self-esteem. I acknowledge my priorities and God's power, potential, promise and presence within me. Therefore, I do not spend major time on minor things or with minor people. I have learned to tell all negative, gossipy, critical, judgmental and dream-stomping people to "kiss my positive attitude."

(10) I recall a funny, yet revealing line in the movie "Steel Magnolias" with Sally Fields, Dolly Parton and Shirley Maclaine. Shirley Maclaine's character was always cranky, rude and anti-social. When confronted about her disposition, she replied, "I'm not crazy I've just been in a *bad mood* for 40 years."

Well, sisters, how many of us have been in a bad mood for 10, 20, 30, 40 years? People may misjudge you and think you are rude, mean, cold-hearted and cynical. Maybe you're just burned out and in a bad mood because of the lack of self-care and self-love. All of your ills can't be solved in one answer, one pill, one more cookie, another drink, another new outfit or even a man.

Why not treat yourself to a women's retreat in the mountains, near the ocean, out of town, at a beautiful hotel or a spa/resort. If budget or time don't permit this on a regular basis, take a long hot soothing bath with candles, aromas, and beautiful music. Turn off your phone and pager.

In counseling with women who are burned out, stressed out and stretched to the limit, I often learn they only take showers. This is indicative of women in a hurry and on-the-run. Slow down, pamper yourself, breathe, cry, pray, sing, hum and allow yourself the gift of the healing water and peace.

Every year since 1986 I have offered a women's retreat

either in the mountains, LaCosta Spa/resort or Palm Springs. It is a gift I give myself. Even though I am facilitating the weekend, I also play and rest. I look forward to them every year. Locate my contact address and number in the back of the book to learn when the next retreat is scheduled. You deserve it!

(11) Pay attention to your nutritional lifestyle. Can you reduce any drinking, smoking, fatty foods, meat, sodas, sweets, fast foods? I recommend reading Queen Afua's book Heal Thyself as a guide for proper fasting.

(12) Re-evaluate your life....no matter how much it hurts. Maybe denial and choosing escapes like staying busy, sleeping too much or ignoring "signs" in your health, relationships, career or spending behavior are catching up with you. Re-evaluate your life. Have your values changed....are you commuting too many hours for a paycheck....when was your last medical check up....is it time for that "talk" with someone....when was the last time you laughed....are you tired, depressed or angry all the time....are you hiding from the bill collectors....are you stuck in a rut?

Denial creates pent up pressure. Act before it's too late. What you resist....persists. When we resist change <u>and</u> anything that is meant for your well-being....pain is the result. Blockages to growth are dis-ease. There is no ease in your health, finances, career, faith or relationships.

What are some of the most common blockages? They are Fear, Procrastination, Ignorance, Hatred, Selfishness, Dishonesty, Low Self-Esteem and Wrong associations. Being stubborn or full of pride and ego is a blockage to your success and well being. All of these are enemies within. Say out loud the word, "En - e - my." It sounds like "in me." That's where the blockages are to your peace of mind and success....in you....not outside of you.

If you wait until you're *sick and tired* of a condition in your life to make a change or improve and act....you'll probably be <u>too</u> sick and tired to make the right choices. The downward spiral will just continue. So choose to evolve. Choose a preventive/productive lifestyle.

Some people change from desperation while others evolve from inspiration. When you evolve in consciousness, it affects your behavior. What you think, believe and feel influence how you act. As you are inspired and evolve, your behavior patterns make it is easier to make decisions, correct, let go, move on and move through fear.

It's more difficult to evolve and create positive changes when you are in the midst of a crisis all the time….broke, lonely, depressed, needy, overwhelmed, burned out, sick and tired. So do the self-inventory and review your lifestyle for necessary realignment with your divine purpose and values before that happens. Your peace of mind is worth it.

Time Out
by Jewel Diamond Taylor

I'm tired of dealing with less, mess and stress.
Just once I don't want to know the how, when,
        what, where or who.
I just need time….with nothing to do.
I don't want to hear any questions, pagers, traffic or phones.
I need to hear my own inner voice.
I need to be alone.
I'm not being mean, selfish or lazy
        but if I don't stop….I think I'll go crazy.
Don't ask me if I'm trying too hard or tell me I'm being
        too sensitive or weak.
I'm giving myself permission to exhale and find me.
I don't want to try to convince, control
        or try to figure things out.
I just need some *time* out.

My get up and go has got up and went.
My energy, time and money is spent.
There are so many people and things that I miss.
Like Momma, laughter, the ocean, dancing at parties
        and a long sweet kiss.

Excuse me while I go inside myself
    even though it may be dark and full of illusions.
But believe me this gift of peace I give myself
    will renew me and remove all confusion.
Don't feel insecure or responsible for my happiness
    while I'm away inside of my temporary blue mood.
Excuse me while I taste my tears and some of Spirit's food.

I'll be back out again soon...
    but right now I have to *go in.*

ENJOY YOUR SILENCE

Women are wanted by men and children for so many reasons. Women are nurturers, caregivers, wife, lover, sister, daughter, Mommy, taxi driver, nurse, healer, therapist, disciplinarian, cook, maid, decorator, provider, tutor, peace maker, prayer warrior....and these are just some of the many hats she wears in the household alone. More women today live further from their core family, living with issues of rising costs, unstable economy, changing workforce, head of household, poor child care, housing, medical and educational services, demanding relationships and careers, feelings overworked, underpaid and unappreciated.

Sisterfriends, you and I have a lot of different issues that need attention and healing. So many problems require so many different *soul*utions to soothe that mind, body and soul which yearns for stability, security, beauty and wholeness.

105

Your body deserves, performs and feels better when you give it healthy food, lots of water, fruits and vegetables, exercise, fresh air, quality clothes, hugs, tenderness, beauty, peace, positive thoughts, beautiful scenery, soothing music, healing massages, pedicure, manicure, shoes that fit, less stress, cleanliness and order, wonderful aromas and scents, herbal and vitamin supplements (calcium, iron, minerals, cascara sagrada, black cohosh, alfalfa, wheat grass, spirulina), take those tight pants, tight girdles, tight bras, tight belts and tight shoes off, mediate, exhale, breathe deeply and enjoy your own silence, buy yourself some flowers, write a "thank you" note to yourself to acknowledge your strength, sacrifice, endurance, beauty, intelligence, small or big accomplishments, faith, service, compassion, and love; decorate your home and wardrobe with vibrant colors, wear your jewelry that sparkles, even if it is a *"fake it 'till you make it"* diamond ring! Treat yourself like a queen. Sisterfriends let's rise and shine!

Make a promise to yourself to review my "Self-Care Goals and Promises" checklist often. Gradually incorporate these practices into your calendar and budget. You are worthy. You are a queen!

SELF-CARE AFFIRMATION

I promise to take good care of my total well-being. Without excuses, blame, hesitation or apology....I joyfully and proactively work on improving my mind, body, emotions, relationships, career, finances, dreams, self-esteem and spiritual joy.

SELF-CARE GOALS AND PROMISES

__pedicure

__manicure

__hair

__facial

__mammogram

__pap smear

__dental care

__eye care/glasses

__drink more water

__listen to favorite music

__write poetry

__vacation/retreat

__mental health day off from work

__massage, reflexology

__buy myself a gift (art, camera, jewelry, computer)

__brighten, redecorate, re-organize home or work area

__savings account

__new undergarments (bra, gowns, panties, stockings)

__take myself on a date

__special interest class

__read more books

__attend more concerts

__clean out closets

__buy a new purse/wallet

__replenish makeup/skin care items

__ shoes, accessories

__health/nutrition

__sugar reduced

__meditate and act upon my inner voice regarding my divine purpose

__write in my journal

__write down my goals

__start a creative project

__update resume/skills/ education

__visit/renew friendships

__exercise/recreation

BIG GIRLS DO CRY SOMETIMES

Sisters, we can admit that even though we are career women, strong women, praying women, survivors of pain, head of the household putting food on the table, negotiators at the corporate table, CEOs, MDs, or VIPs, policy makers, movers and shakers....at times we are fragile, frightened, unsure of ourselves and need comforting and reassurance....yet we are told:

Be strong, you're the oldest

Be tough you've got that corporate job

Don't complain, you're married, you shouldn't have any problems

Be strong, you're single and head of the household

Bear up, you can make it even if you've just lost your husband, your mother, your child, your best friend, your job, your home, or your business

You shouldn't complain, you have everything
you don't need any help, you're always so "together"

You don't need any more friends, you're so popular already

You always seem to cope and adapt, you'll be all right by yourself

You'll work it out, you always bounce back

Since you're always helping others....I didn't think you needed any help. I didn't think you'd mind that I forgot your birthday, your recent loss, your recent accomplishment...you're not sensitive, you don't need any attention...you're sufficient

There is still a "little girl" inside of that grown-up woman. Sometimes women appear so strong, competent, resilient, popular and powerful....that people around them assume they don't require the thoughtful reaffirming gestures of friendship and love. There are women who wear the mask and cape of "superwoman" organizing, cleaning, shopping, cooking, caregiving, rescuing others, creating and working faster than a speeding bullet, leaping over a stack of laundry baskets and bills in a single bound. Sometimes the isolation is self-imposed because she hasn't been used to delegating duties, self-care or allowing others through her emotional wall.

If you're one of those kind of women who feel unsure, fragile, unappreciated and about to cry at any moment....it's time to stop the merry-go-round. It's OK to say, I need to breathe, regroup, go on a retreat, laugh again, seek help or be comforted.

For too long women have been socially conditioned to feel that they are being selfish if they develop self-esteem and the courage to say "no" to anyone or any activity that is causing her to feel forgotten, unappreciated, misunderstood or burned out.

I have found it very healing and reaffirming to allow myself to be vulnerable every once in a while and admit my hurts. I let my sisterfriends come over my emotional wall by telling them my needs. It's amazing how much we all have in common when we break down those walls. Many of us have "been there, done that" or even "still there, going through it right now."

I'm not suggesting that you go out and tell all your business and invite everyone to your pity party. But in time, trust your judgement and opportunity to share with another sisterfriend. It might be an elder, a sister in your support group, book club or the one you always confide in. You might find out it was just what she needed too....a good cry and a good laugh.

DON'T LET DEPRESSION WIN

Now more than ever, women are working outside of the home and coming home to continue working as the homemaker too. When she becomes overwhelmed she doesn't have time for a breakdown. But she will continue working and functioning on a minimum level. She's masquerading and her smile looks out of place. As Smokey Robinson wrote, "if you look a little closer, you'd see the tracks of my tears."

Depression is more likely to happen to a woman who is isolated because of lack of transportation, friends and family living far away or she is not in a satisfying relationship. A sense of belonging derived from family and friendships provides the emotional support that keeps her feeling secure, valued and connected. Sisters today are going back to the "old school" way of women gathering. At retreats, in homes, book clubs and conferences, women are gathering, sharing, reading healing, praying, and networking. They are seeking answers on how to positively cope with illness, relationships, setbacks, parenting, self-esteem, and spiritual joy.

As a busy, traveling career woman I found myself missing the comfort and conversation of my sisterfriends. I started inviting sisters to my home each month for what I call "Sister Saturday." It is our sacred, special and private time for sharing. We dress casual, no children, no formality. We share food, laughter, testimonies, questions, poems, creative ideas and go for a group walk. We find we have so much in common. It became so popular that now I'm invited to facilitate my "Sister Saturday" in other sister's homes. We're discovering we are not alone in our frustrations and poor coping skills. The fast pace life of commuting, balancing career and relationships, demands of motherhood, being in the choir, serving on committees, going to school and looking for love in all the wrong places has left a void in many of our lives.

Our mothers and grandmothers used to sit on the front porches talking. They shared in childcare responsibilities, laughter and tears. Multi-generations lived together under one roof or at least lived down the street. Interdependence was the glue that shaped our commUNITY. Integration changed all that. Families and friends moved away from each other. Now miles and busy agendas separate us. Integration contributed to the isolation we experience today. Isolation breeds depression.

Now we communicate by faxes, caller I.D., voice mail,

pagers, and e-mail. Technology may have offered conveniences but it created a society of people always in a hurry and too busy for the personal and emotional connections that soothe the soul. Men and women today are coping with minor and major life challenges alone. We have blended families, a higher divorce rate, more single mothers and women in crisis with AIDS, in prison, unemployed, struggling with substance abuse, domestic abuse, and trying to recover from financial problems. People are choosing destructive coping behavior to face each mountain.

From my own personal victories out of my valleys of depression I have learned some very positive insights about coping with it. After each "Sister Saturday" in my home I am reaffirmed, comforted and rejuvenated. I've been in the company of my sisters. Each time, I let go of some stress and acquire new insight. We all feel more connected, stronger and wiser.

In my travels as a speaker, retreat facilitator and counselor, I have heard some incredible testimonies of endurance, faith, recovery and self-care attitudes. Women are seeking answers to improve their parenting, self-esteem, career satisfaction, health issues and relationships. They want to know how to navigate their lives through the waters that are unfamiliar and ever changing. Women are pulling themselves out of the dark holes of depression and life-styles that are harmful and unproductive

Sisters need to know that they can avoid drowning in their misery. Feelings of shame, guilt, fear and hopelessness are emotions that take one on a downward spiral. There are positive and redemptive insights that can serve as a life pre-server to keep someone from drowning in that misery. My soul has been anchored from maturing in my spiritual faith and learning the lessons of life. As food for thought, I toss out these ideas to hold onto to keep one's head above water.

(1) Don't resist what you're feeling and beat yourself up emo-tionally. You can't always predict, control or change people and circumstances. Life brings us seasons but not always reasons.

(2) Being a workaholic and/or driven by material success can get you out of balance. Comparing and competing decreases self-esteem and inner peace. When a goal isn't realized, don't give up. Sometimes setbacks are a reset button to cause you to act and choose again wiser. Begin again with a new plan and new faith.

(3) Happiness and contentment are not in acquisitions....it's an attitude.

(4) Check your surroundings. You'll recover better with uplifting, peaceful, and creative influences around you.

(5) Some people lean and some people lift. Choose your friends and mate carefully.

(6) Don't allow yourself to be paralyzed by anger, bitterness or hopelessness. The past has passed. In due time you need to get up and get over it! Let it go. God forgives and forgets....can you?

(7) Your immune system is vulnerable when you are stressed and depressed. Eat more healthy nutritious foods. Have therapeutic massages regularly.

(8) If you are normally a very active person, then be still for a while, collect your thoughts, meditate, pray, rest and allow fresh new ideas and energy to come into your mind, heart and soul. If you are normally inactive, it's time to get up, change your scenery, go for a walk, exercise, enjoy nature.

(9) Stress and depression can distort reality. Don't overreact and create more drama for yourself. Change your focus and conversation and your feelings will follow. Start by counting your blessings. Remember you are TOO blessed to be stressed.

(10) Know that God's grace, love and mercy are yours. You are worthy, divine and stronger than you probably realize. Feelings of fear, shame and guilt will block your blessings and peace of mind. You may need some time alone for awhile. But when it's necessary, don't be afraid to ask for help. Don't shut yourself off from family, friends and activities that give you joy. You are NOT the only one who will experience delays, defeats and disappointments. This, TOO, shall pass!

10

WHEN IS LOVE BLIND?

Whenever sisterfriends sit around the table, if the confidence and comfort factor is there, we talk about our stupid mistakes and blind love that didn't see the writing on the wall. No matter what age or socio-economic level, women are still taking men to the *altar* hoping to *alter* them just because they saw some potential.

Sisters young and old, out of neediness, loneliness, ignorance, immaturity, and "spiritual retardation" are still finding themselves in unhappy, unfulfilling, toxic and unequally yoked relationships.

We need to continue to seek wisdom and learn lessons about the difference between what is *lust, love* or just *liking* a man. Discernment, discipline and the ability to detect the signs of behavior that are warning signs can save us a lot of heartache. Yet we still proceed thinking it will go away, we can change them, it's alright for now, it's the best we can do, don't want to be alone....the rationalizations are too numerous to list.

Food, drugs, shopping, alcohol, being a workaholic, and looking for love in all the wrong places are temporary pain killers that destroy and diminish us. Only we can stop the cycle of pain in our families of seeing our Mothers, Aunties, daughters and sisterfriends and *ourselves* from repeatedly *"falling"* in love instead of growing in love. We fall into wrong relationships, and it takes years of recovery, and a toll on our children, our health, self-esteem, finances and spirituality.

There is a cost and loss when we ignore, rationalize, justify or don't see the warning signs—those red flags—in a man's behavior that tells us he has different values, married, attracted to other men, secretive, manipulative, abusive, sexually unsatisfying, untrustworthy, always late, rude, loud, non-committed, not intellectually politically, spiritually, economically or emotionally compatible, violent, hot tempered, moody, has a drug/alcohol problem, immature, poor hygiene, selfish, poor money manager, lacks parenting or family values, disrespectful to his Mother or other females in his family. We are blind to these negative personality traits when we are needy, immature, lack discipline and have low self-esteem.

It takes time, study and unconditional love just to know, accept and appreciate our own personalities.

Sisterfriends, as we continue on the path of self-awareness, self-esteem and spiritual obedience, we are healing ourselves. The goal is to become whole women instead of a hurting women attracting and accepting more hurt and disappointment.

We can look at relationships in our family and around us that have failed and learn what NOT to do. We can study the quality, not just quantity in years of working, loving relationships. What keeps couples together....could it be a sense of humor, shared common values, communication, praying together, the ability to forgive, letting each other know how important and loved they are, balance of time with work and family? Relationships and marriages are like fire....they go out, if not attended to.

A man falls in love with his *eyes*. A woman falls in love with her *ears*. So if he wants to keep us, he has to keep *saying* those wonderful, flattering, praising compliments, for we are motivated by what we *hear*. This also explains why women often think a man loves her, because he *says* "all the right things," at the beginning. Then when his actions don't match the words spoken, disillusionment and pain set in. She begins to realize the relationship is built on shaky ground.

Men are motivated by a woman's *physical* appearance first. If it is real geniune unconditional love, it builds on her other assets of intelligence, spirituality, compatibility, etc. But if the attraction is shallow and purely sexual, it doesn't grow beyond what he *sees*. If the woman gets too comfortable with the relationship and begins to neglect her appearance, the attraction and relationship is ended.

Every woman isn't meant to be a wife or a mother. Some women get married to have children because of society and family pressures. If you talk to most single women, they want to get married because they feel they're missing out on something - many married women wish they were single, because they feel they're missing out on something.

One would think, with the explosion of information, support groups, open discussions, women's magazines, books, tapes and counseling available for self-esteem, parenting, relationships and matters of the heart, the cycle of pain would diminish. In spite of all the education and support—teen pregnancy, domestic abuse, emotionally wounded children from broken and divorced homes are still alarmingly high.

Sisterfriends, we are charged with the responsibility to "know thyself"...."love thyself"...."respect thyself".... "develop thyself" and "educate thyself." By doing this we are creating a healthy, mature and worthy mindset to attract, maintain and sustain the kind of divine, soul-full, rewarding, loving, compatible, affirming, and sacred relationship we deserve.

11

WHY ARE BLACK MEN SO ANGRY?

Men and women are "wired" emotionally different. Men and women think about love, sex, relationships, money, family, and self-image in different ways. Men are traditionally conditioned for *action, hunting, warrior, protector, provider, competitive, winning and conquering.* A man's value is measured by how he performs in the work place, the boardroom and the bedroom. His physical strength and tough warrior-like skills are heightened as opposed to his sensitive side or communications skills.

Women are traditionally conditioned for *gathering, community/family building, child rearing, emotionally expressive, nurturing, reactive and socially aware.* Therefore, our interpersonal skills are heightened early. We are more in touch with our *fee*lings (fe*male*) and usually better communicators.

So often the division between men and women is

widened because we communicate differently, we cope with external and internal issues differently. *Women* tend to *internalize* their pain and emotions thereby resulting in depression, ulcers, tumors, headaches, arthritis, overeating, overspending and other self-destructive behavior.

Men tend to *externalize* their pain and emotions resulting in more visible manifestations. Their anger can be seen by loud talking, fighting, heart attacks, violence, abuse of women, graffitti, excessive drinking, or drugs.

Both men and women need to develop positive, healthy and constructive ways to cope with anger, hurt, racism, rejection, grief, and disappointments in life.

Sisters, we think that because our coping skills are more subtle, less obvious and discriminating, it is better. But our ways can bring about that same destructive end. Whether the anger is internalized or externalized, *if it continues,* it is certainly dangerous for all concerned. Anger is just one letter short of d*anger.* Sometimes we don't understand why our fathers, husbands, sons, lovers and male co-workers are angry and seem to take it out on us. We see too many of them losing their jobs, locked down in jails, killing one another, wasting their talent and lives away with alcohol and drugs or—their anger is suppressed, therefore, rather than fight, feel, communicate or confront it....they waste precious hours sitting in front of the television.

Their anger may….or may not be justifiable. Perhaps if we looked at some of the reasons Black men say they are angry….we are better prepared to understand it, diffuse it, avoid it, heal it and decrease it.

BLACK MEN ARE ANGRY BECAUSE....

(1) He has unresolved resentment with his parent(s). (abandonment, rejection, made to feel inadequate and insecure)

(2) He hates his job and feels stuck.

(3) He has no power on his job, so he exerts it at home.

(4) He experiences racism at the job and on the streets.

(5) He was rejected, betrayed, unappreciated in a previous relationship, distrusts all women.

(6) He is sexually confused or secretive about his sexual orientation.

(7) He was sexually abused as a child.

(8) He feels inadequate, ashamed of lack of education.

(9) He expected a son, disappointed with having a daughter.

(10) He's angry because his wife doesn't work or make enough money, he feels overwhelmed or that it is unfair to burden the financial responsibility.

(11) He feels trapped in the marriage.

(12) He hasn't learned how to....or doesn't feel safe to express his real feelings, he feels that sharing his pain, weakens him as a man.

Your experiences could probably add to the list. As nurturers we tend to think we can fix it, stop it or endure it. But as conscious women, we need to know that we do not have to be silent targets, martyrs, volunteer victims or enablers of men's anger.

Dysfunctional families, an unhappy childhood, failed relationships and racism are a reality. All of us are responsible and accountable for our behavior though. No one should continue blaming others for their lack of emotional mastery. Anger is only purposeful when it mobilizes us to effect change and to act and find a way to stop that which is causing the anger. Beneath all anger is *pain*. When someone feels hurt, unloved, ignored, put down, invisible, violated or disappointed....anger is the result. If the source of the pain isn't dealt with....either the anger grows out of control.....or the anger is suppressed and denied. In both cases it is detrimental. When the pain is healed....then the anger goes away.

Not seeing or acknowledging someone's faults or pain is just as bad as not seeing or acknowledging their goodness and value. Men and women are suffering and in need of information and support to enhance their relationships. Pointing the finger at each other and closing our minds certainly won't help. Anger, betrayal, racism, broken hearts and loneliness aren't exclusive to one gender. Self-awareness, self-correction and positive dialogue with solutions as the objective are the steps toward creating more passionate, compatible and lasting relationships.

Women talking about the mystery, mistakes and myths about men, sex, love, dating, marriage and breaking up will always be a major curiosity and a source of debate. How do we avoid the trap? How do we discern the good from the bad? How do we maintain a relationship? How do we let go of the unfulfilling ones? What are women doing right to attract good men? What are women doing wrong to lose a man's interest, respect and passion? Sisters, I can imagine as you talk in beauty shops, on retreats, in your book clubs, during women ministry groups, teaching your daughters, or confiding in your girlfriend....you can arrive at some interesting theories.

I was fortunate to meet a young brotherfriend from Houston, Texas, named William July, II. He is the author of the best-seller book Brothers, Lust and Love. Reading his book was insightful, daring, truthful and humorous. I thought it would be helpful for the sisterfriends to hear from the brothers' point of view, some answers to our questions. With his gracious permission, I include one of his chapters....

10 WAYS TO DRIVE HIM AWAY

Some women don't know it, but they're driving the men they love right out of their lives. I'm not a psychologist or relationship expert. But that's precisely why I'm qualified to write about this subject. Statistics, theories, and "expert" opinions have been stated on the matter. But nobody has asked the ordinary everyday hard working brother on the street what he thinks. After all, isn't he the man all of these brilliant experts claim to know so much about?

For a change, I asked the real men what they thought. None of these men were from the hallowed halls of academia. None of them are sociologists, psychologists, or relationship experts. They're just regular guys. Some of the ordinary men consulted were a computer technician, a personal fitness trainer, a mail courier, a college student, an entrepreneur, a corporate executive, a sanitation worker, a police officer, a mechanic, and an attorney.

The question to them was, "What are some things women do that drive men away?" I asked them to be blunt and candid. However, I first prefaced my question to them with the fact that it wasn't intended to be a list of random gripes. Instead, this is a list of things that men wished women knew. The intention of this list is to attempt to avoid some problems before they occur. Or to at least bring them out into the open for discussion. Most of their answers kept coming back to variations of the ten areas explained below.

1. Acting Sweet to get a Man, Then Changing

"I don't know why women act so sweet during dating and change completely when they know they've got you."

Alvin-Computer Technician.

She used to go to bed in a naughty nighty and didn't care about sweating the curls out of her head. Now she goes to bed with a head full of rollers and a face covered with Noxema. When they were dating, she batted her eyes, spoke softly, and always looked sexy. But now that she's got him, that has all changed. No more gently batting eyes and shy smiles. Those have been replaced with frowns, pursed lips, and shrill tones. No more sexy clothes. Now she dresses like she doesn't care what she looks like; every day is a bad hair day, and she's fast going from pleasantly plump to a pig.

Of course, men can't expect women to be superwomen who are able to work, cook, clean, and screw with flawless precision. But a woman shouldn't start out playing the superwoman role at the beginning and then change. It's better to present herself as she is and get it all out in the open. When a woman changes her entire act after the relationship gets going, men feel as though they've been duped into believing a lie. Suddenly, he doesn't know what to believe anymore. What happened to the woman he fell in love with?

2. Not Giving Enough Space

"She clings to me because she thinks that every minute I'm not with her I'm fooling around."

     Lewis - Personal Fitness Trainer.

     The "S" word must be used carefully. Admittedly, some men intentionally abuse the term space to cover intentions to fool around while not giving up what they already have. But not all are that way. Most men simply just want some room to be themselves. Men need to feel that they aren't trapped or being held hostage in their lives. To do this, from time to time, men want to get away and be alone or hang out with their friends.

     But it's straining on the relationship when women think that a man is being selfish, silly, or making up an excuse to go out and cheat just because he wants some space. The smart woman knows that a man wants his space and doesn't trample over his need for it. On the other hand, jealous and possessive women are well known for their deliberate attempts to invade

WHY ARE BLACK MEN SO ANGRY?

and conquer a man's privacy. Those are the women who think letting a man out of their sight is a mistake. They keep chokeholds on their men and eventually drive them away. But if she can't give the man a little space, either the relationship isn't solid or she has some personal problems she need to deal with. If it's because she can't trust him out of her sight, she doesn't need that man anyway.

3. Wanting too Many Things

"I'm just a working man. I can't afford a two story house in the suburbs, not to mention the Lexus, the Range Rover, a bunch of credit cards, and kids too."

> Jesse - Mail Courier.

Many Black men say Black women want too much. Of course, wanting a good hard working man who respects women isn't asking too much. But what about when it goes beyond that? For some women, having a good man just isn't enough. They also want a Lexus, a two story in the suburbs, and a string of credit cards. When they don't have these things they moan and complain as though life is terrible. If the man dares to say something about how he's happy with things as they are, he'll be accused of being complacent, lazy, and lacking ambition. It's all right to have goals and want some luxuries, but an assessment of the blessings you already have never hurts either.

4. Not Saying What She Means

"Women expect you to read their minds like a psychic."

Jamal-College Student.

Men aren't very good mind readers. In fact, we have enough difficulty just figuring out what women mean with the words they speak. Also, I dare say women are far more sophisticated communicators than men. They seem to be more adept at the subtleties of gestures, facial expressions, and body language. Therefore, men and women almost always suffer from communication blackouts in relationships.

It seems that, regardless of what their mouths are saying, women are more apt to use voice inflections and body language to say what they really mean. Take this statement for example: "No, I don't mind if you go out with your friends instead of taking me to a movie tonight." She says this while tapping her foot and looking away with her arms folded. Although, her mouth said quite literally, "No, I don't mind," she probably expected him to read her non-verbal cues.

If he fails to detect her undertone of disapproval and her body language, he'll find himself in an argument later about the very same incident. His attitude will be, "What's the problem?" To which she'll respond, "You know what the problem is." That will go on for several rounds. At the end of the fight there will be a split decision as to who the winner is.

The woman believes that the man is just so callous and selfish that he refuses to admit that he was wrong. Likewise, the man will be thinking that she's nagging for no reason. Both of them will go to bed angry.

A Word to the Wise: In the section, "Not Saying What She Means," I am not talking about the issue of sexual consent. If a man doesn't want to find himself in prison, he'd better realize that no really means no.

5. The Three B's of Sex

"I'm going to be straight about it. The sex is important to me."

Gene - Entrepreneur.

I wish we were all so spiritually evolved that sex didn't matter. But don't look for that development during your lifetime. Sex is a big part of a relationship. It's probably more important than it should be. Basically the sexual aggravations of men in a relationship boil down to the three B's: Bad, Boring, and Boudoir Battle.

Bad Sex - Sex is a learned skill. It's similar to driving a car. Basically, anyone can do it. Some are good at it. And others are experts. But everyone has an idea of what they consider good and bad sex. Common complaints among men are lack of enthusiasm, lack of rhythm, no creativity, and poor technique. It's something that should be intelligently and honestly discussed by a couple. The reasons for such problems could be psychological, physical, ethical, religious, or a host of other considerations and professional counseling may even be necessary in some cases.

Boring Sex - Boring sex isn't necessarily the same thing as bad sex. But it is far from good. Boring sex is the same old place, same old hour of the evening, and same position, every time. It's when the sex feels more like service than a desire. Boring sex is when you're going through all the motions, but there's no spice or passion involved.

Boudoir Battle - Using sex as a weapon doesn't work to do anything but make a man angry. It can be subtle things such as not being warm to touching and cuddling. Or it can be more strategic. It can be the refusal to do certain things in bed. The most brutal form of bedroom battle is outright refusal. We all know that technique doesn't work today. Too many other women are ready, willing, and able to step up and take the place of the woman who is refusing.

Of course, a man can't expect a woman who is angry at him to make mad passionate love to him. That's where communication comes into play. It's far better to talk and resolve the differences than to play games of will because any real man will be very insulted by this. Then he may become vengeful and the whole thing turns into a cold war of revenge.

6. Constantly Talking About Other Men

"She's always talking about this guy at her job and it really pisses me off."

Sean - Corporate Executive.

Men don't like to hear women constantly talking about other men. It's not necessarily an ego problem. It's just that each man wants to feel special and important to the woman in his life. Women don't have to cradle us like babies. Nor do they need to be patronizing. But a woman would be wise to realize that the ego of a man can be fragile. This is particularly true with Black males as we are constantly attempting to gain and maintain the basic elements of American manhood: the ability to provide, protect, and be masters of our of own destinies.

7. Being a Drama Queen

"She calls my pager all day when I'm at work. Then when I call her back, she just starts whining about some little thing that could've waited until later."

Art - Sanitation Worker.

Drama queens are always whining, pestering, or nagging about something. With them, nothing can ever be right. They pull all kinds of little tricks to get and control a man's attention. If he's watching television, she wants him to get up and put out the trash. When he has time off from work, she tries to plan each hour of those days for him. If it's bill paying time, she's crying about her car note being late. Some of them have a well developed damsel in distress act that they play to get a man's attention. The Drama Queen is always saying "save me." Initially it may make a man feel good to be the chivalrous knight in shining armor. But too much distress can drive even the most loyal knight to ride off into the sunset.

8. Being Hard and Cold

"I work the grave yard shift so I don't have to be at home with my wife."

        Derek - Police Officer.

        That response was from a man who had been married less than one year. He and his wife were already engaged in a cold war. She was being openly disrespectful to him as a human being, not just as a man. Other times she was cold and aloof, barely acknowledging that he was in the room. Believe it or not, men have feelings too. Hard and cold behavior is enough to drive anyone away. Again we aren't asking to be cradled like babies, but every man wants home to be a safe refuge from the cold-hearted world, and when the world at home is colder than the work world, there is no solace.

134

9. Cheating

"They call us dogs but women are out there fooling around just as much."

Barry - Auto Mechanic.

I've talked to women who will swear up and down that when a woman is cheating it's always the fault of a man. That simply isn't true. Women are human beings and are therefore just as subject to dishonesty and deceit as any man. If there were no men on earth, cheating wouldn't cease to exist.

Cheating takes two forms. First, there's the obvious form which is having affairs. But the second way of cheating is mental. It's the subtle form of getting over. She may not be fooling around with another man but she may be cheating by fooling around with the balance of the checkbook. Her body may be faithful, but she may be cheating by playing manipulative games to keep him within her control. Those games rob him of his energy and creativity and thus he's being cheated of realizing his full growth potential. The truth is that cheating doesn't have to be about affairs or lovers. Cheating is deceit and that can take many forms.

10. Power Struggle

"I can't stand it when a woman always want to prove to me that she's smart, tough, and independent."

Lawrence - Attorney.

135

Don't misunderstand this one. Constantly competing doesn't include the fact that a woman may have a more successful career, more money, a better car, or more education than the man in her life. Likewise, it isn't the assumption that a man should possess all the power in a relationship. Constantly competing is the old immature "you can't tell me what to do" attitude. It's very irritating. Especially to a man who isn't trying to tell her what to do.

Other ways women constantly compete are: (1) Making sure they look smarter than a man by intentionally upstaging him in public. (2) Disagreement for the sake of disagreement. (3) Unnecessary rudeness. (4) Being condescending and cutting down what he says when he states his personal thoughts and opinions.

I know this list is going to make the tempers of some women flare. But this isn't a list of complaints. It's a list of information intended to provoke thoughts and spark dialogue. Instead of getting angry, talk about these things with your husband, the man in your life, or a male friend. In doing so, you might make things for both of you a little better.

12

RELATIONSHIPS

More and more books, discussions, sermons and lectures are discussing the secrets and steps to a happy relationship. Men and women bring so much from their childhood and past relationships to a new one. If emotional issues are not healed, they surface again in the new relationship. Relationships are mirrors. They are teachers that teach us about our weaknesses and our strengths.

Women are more likely to lose themselves of the inner demons of guilt, shame, secrets and past transgressions (abortion, adultery, addictions, abuse, childhood pain, fears, stress, and spiritual battle). When a man admits his fears or past, he is called a whimp, too sensitive, weak, or a punk. On the other hand, women will talk it through, cry, seek counseling, read, reform, resist peer pressure, let it go and give it to God. Sisters....we have magazines, books, clubs, churches, support groups, sisterfriends, conferences, retreats, etc. These outlets are educational, comforting and healing. What support systems do men have? Men are conditioned to be the warriors, providers, survivors and to hold in their emotions. There's no time, in his mind, for inner battle because he's constantly on the battlefield of employment, racism, violence, pride, peer pressure, ego, thrill seeking and competition. His identity comes from how much money he makes, where he works, what kind of car he drives and the women in his life.

A woman's identity is usually defined by her relationships, appearance, children and home. Society gives women permission to cry, ask for help or just take time off. Men are told to "keep going, don't tell your problems, handle your business and handle your woman."

A man may secretly yearn for closeness, a stronger marriage or learn how to be more romantic, sensitive and responsive in his relationship. But to attend a class on relationships, go to counseling or buy books about relationships is somehow telling the world that he is weak. When he's stressed, tired, wants to tune out the world, or tune out you, he doesn't know how or doesn't want to engage in verbal battle with you. He'll just sit in front of the television for hours to escape. Or like most men prone to externalize their emotions, he'll work hard or play hard. It's safer and acceptable to act out than to feel what's inside. Some men will cope with stress and anger by talking loud, wrecking the car, beating the wife and kids, excessive drinking, physical activity (sports, sex, workaholic). Men are more action-orientated while women are more feel-ing orientated. Maybe that's why we are called FEmale.

A woman tends to center her life around relationships while men tend to center their priorities around work, money, power and status. As little girls, we were being prepared for relationships playing with dolls, reading bridal magazines and fairy tales with happy endings. We were talking, crying, laugh-ing, playing, dreaming, studying and in some cases pampered. Little boys were fighting, reading "girlie" magazines, experi-menting with sex, missing class and playing games. A lot of them learned how to be players on and off the field.

Those little boys and little girls both grew up unpre-pared for mature relationships. Sisters....we thought we were falling in love but we really fell into reality. The intimacy (into mate) that you crave of emotional connecting with your mate perhaps isn't there because generally speaking, men were not taught how to be a friend and lover to a woman. And let's be fair, most young women, then and now, aren't taught how to be a friend and lover to her man. He is taught to act and women are taught to attract. Society and family fed "him" and "her" poor examples, myths, media images and fairy tales about their gender roles and expectations.

We can't take someone to the altar and hope to alter that person. Both people go into a relationship with expectations, dreams, shortcomings, strengths, and emotional baggage.

There is so much to learn and so much to unlearn. We learn from examples, education and experience. We need to break generational cycles of pain, divorce, abuse, infidelity, and unsatisfying relationships. Are there positive relationships around you that inspire you to provide healthy and loving examples of two people who have respect, communication, forgiveness, honesty, a sense of humor, mutual support, shared interests, love, trust, cooperation and spiritually yoked?

Relationships are stronger when both are in agreement and in communication with four books.

(1) The Checkbook for financial harmony and prosperity. Sharing common financial goals, planning and spending behavior will minimize distrust, secrets and financial ruin.

(2) Cookbook for sharing meals regularly and having common food preferences and life-styles that can lead to good health and longevity.

(3) The Goodbook for spiritual harmony, faith, endurance, wisdom and seeking God's grace and direction for all matters.

(4) <u>Phone</u>book for having mutual friends to share social activities and holidays together. You may each have your own friends, but too many separate friendships outside of your relationship can lead to problems.

You and I will grow wiser and stronger as we learn how to recognize and avoid any behavior, treatment, activity, or attitude that keeps us from fulfilling relationships. I read some interesting comments about relationships from the Editor-In-Chief of <u>Heart and Soul</u> Magazine, Stephanie Stokes Oliver. Her comments on relationships are reprinted from the September 1996 issue with her permission.

STEPHANIE STOKES OLIVER

"If you don't believe in love, you may as well not believe in nothing." That's the line from August Wilson's latest Broadway play, <u>Seven Guitars</u>. Don't you think that's pretty good philosophy? I do. Romantic at heart that I am, I truly believe in love. To have a loving, supportive, healthy relationship in your life is a wonderful blessing. Having loved a few brothers myself and having been married to the most special one for 16 years, I've collected a bunch of little philosophies about love. Here are a few of them:

It takes a smart woman to find a good man. *That's*

from the Broadway play, <u>Having Our Say</u>. If Sadie Delany said that when she was 103, it's got to be true.

The key to good relationships is not agreement but, rather, acceptance. *This is something I heard in a sermon and wrote down right away. No two people will ever agree on everything, but we can live together peacefully with mutual acceptance.*

No one can make your life complete but you. *You've got to be happy with yourself before you can create a joyous relationship. It's unrealistic to expect someone else to give your life meaning (or even pay off all your bills). Which leads me to the next point....*

A fiancé is not a financier. *Actually, I had a friend whose fiancé paid off all her bills as an engagement present, but because they had known each other only a couple of months before they got married, the marriage didn't last long. The saying, "Money isn't everything" is no lie.*

There will be valleys and there will be mountains. *That's what our minister told Reginald and me when we got married. I have found this simple statement to be a good way to describe the ups and downs that are bound to happen in any love relationship. When you're in a valley, just think about the tops of those mountains you've reached together, and make your way, step by step, to the next one.*

"Let there be spaces in your togetherness". As many of you may know, that's a quote from The Prophet, by Kahlil Gibran. How many relationships have broken up because one mate said, "I need space?" Too many. When you love being with someone, it's natural to want that good feeling all the time. But we must remember another old adage: "Absence makes the heart grow fonder." (And think of all the stuff you can get done when you have time alone!)

Not all brief love is failed love. Just because you don't end up marrying somebody doesn't mean that the relationship was a failure. From one boyfriend I received the gift of vegetarianism—and a great Afro pick that lasted much longer than our relationship. From another I picked up a passion for travel. When we love, we learn.

Sex is when you don't give a damn; love is when you care. Guess who said that? Barry White. Well, sho' you right, Barry.

Making love means having safer sex. That's my personal philosophy—and that of this magazine. By now you probably know that <u>Heart & Soul</u> will always encourage monogamous relationships and the use of protection against AIDS and other STDs. Anyone who loves you would want you to be loving and living a long time.

143

If someone hits you, he doesn't love you - because love feels good. I heard Oprah Winfrey say this on her show. It's so true. Love shouldn't make you feel threatened or victimized; it should make you feel safe and cared for.

13

PARENTING WITH LOVE, WISDOM AND FAITH

Sisterfriends can I get an "amen" on the statement that "parenting is one the hardest yet can be one of the most rewarding jobs in life?" I've given birth to two sons, my pride and joy, John and Jason. They are now young adult men in college. It turns out we are teachers to each other. I've learned so much about life, about myself and understanding the personalities of men from my sons.

I grew up in a household of women. Being married and having two sons has been a truly enlightening experience. It's been quite a juggling act to balance all the hats on my head as a wife, mother, cook, maid, teacher/tutor, taxi driver, nurse, decorator, shopper, seamstress, and that's just what I do as a homemaker.

As a career woman who wanted to enjoy my family at home and build a career, I was fortunate my husband was an involved and caring father, especially since I wasn't much of a "football/baseball mom" enthusiast when it came to their athletic demands. Loving my children was the easy part, even when their behavior or grades fell short of my expectations. But the wisdom, strength, money and time that is required was the challenge. My family is small and the interaction with other family members (grandparents, aunts, uncles and cousins) was very limited because either they live far away, deceased or busy with their own lives. So my children did not benefit from being around an extended family. Being around multi-generations and family support can be a relief to working parents as well as enrich the children's lives.

Women today are challenged and overwhelmed because of family isolation, lack of childcare, transportation, working two jobs, limited family support, single mother without emotional or financial support from the father, and/or she may lack parenting awareness skills.

One source of information for today's African-American parent is available in the <u>Successful Black Parenting Magazine</u>. Janice Robinson, an African-American sister, is the Sisterpres of this publication based in Philadelphia, Pennsylvania. The following are tips from her workshop presentation on "Raising Successful Black Children."

JANICE ROBINSON

Sisters With Children: *Your family responsibilities are never ending. In order to care for your family's needs, you must first care for yourself. As stewardesses on airlines instruct you to put on your oxygen mask before attempting to put one on your child, you must first get your "life's oxygen" by taking care of your wants and needs. Do something you always wanted to in life but didn't because you are now a parent.*

Sisters Without Children: *Raising children is everybody's business, whether or not you have children yourself. There is always a child that could use your attention. Do you know a single mom that could use an extra hand? Are you an aunt? Teacher? If we are to maintain the village, everyone must do their share to protect our future—the children.*

Single Sisters: *Remember when courting a boyfriend, to limit the time he spends with your children. Yes, he needs to get to know your children, but he doesn't need to be around them all the time. Children tend to misbehave around boyfriends. If he thinks their misbehavior is an everyday act, he may get cold feet.*

Grandmoms: *You have raised your children and now are providing the most important service to your grandchildren, your experiences. Enjoy your status as the village elder. You bring a new perspective to the parenting relationship. If you are parenting again, take one day at a time and take care of yourself.*

POSITIVE PARENTING

In spite of resistance, lack of appreciation or fear of failing as a parent, your child needs the following from parents, relatives, teachers, church and community.

DIRECTION: When to come home, when to go to bed, manners, values, selecting friends, and household responsibilities.

ASSOCIATION: Children need to be around elders, as well as children their own age. Who they associate with influences their minds.

APPRECIATION: Verbal praise should be balanced with rewards of gifts and privileges. Children live up to expectations and crave appreciation and approval.

AFFIRMATION: Letting a child know they are capable, qualified, loved, wanted and important develops a healthy self-esteem.

ATTENTION: Love can be demonstrated by quality time, not just material things. When a child misbehaves or seems distracted, it may be a cry for love and attention.

PROTECTION: Every child deserves the right to a safe, clean and harmonious home. If you know of a child who is abandoned, abused, neglected and uncared for, that child deserves to be helped. Get involved....get help.

OBSERVATION: Watch your child's behavior patterns, know their friends, watch their moods, eating habits and study skills. A drastic change could spell trouble. Keep your ears and eyes open.

PARTICIPATION: Get involved with your child's interests in sports, creativity and school activities. A child remembers into adulthood how much your participation meant to their sense of belonging and pride.

COMMUNICATION: Talk and listen to your child. Make it comfortable for your child to come to you in times of fear or concern. Learn how to handle conflicts in a healthy and mature way. When a parent yells and loses control of their emotions, he/she loses control of the situation.

MODERATION: All rules don't work all the time for everyone. Be flexible and remember no two children are the same. Be moderate in discipline, giving privileges, TV time and rules of the house.

STIMULATION: A child's mind will grow restless, numb or seek negative outlets for their unused energy. Seek ways to direct their energy, time and talent. Music, dance, the arts, museums, story telling, sight seeing, colors, change of environment, a change in routine, or pet care will help to stimulate their young minds.

EXPLORATION: Encourage your child to do different things, meet different people, read, travel, go to the library, explore the world of math and science or even volunteer work learning compassion for others.

MOTIVATION: Remind your child that they're intelligent and can accomplish anything in life with belief, education, service, will power, and self-reliance. Show them you believe in them. Don't discourage their early dreams.

NUTRITION: Children need balanced meals to keep them healthy and strong. Too much sugar will make them hyper and have a low attention span in school. Teach them at a young age about good nutrition and exercise. The best way to teach them about the hazards of a poor diet, drugs, alcohol and smoking is by your good example.

EDUCATION: Teach your child about their heritage, their possibilities, their future and to value education. Read with them, go to the library with them, monitor homework and encourage higher education after high school. Teach your **"whole"** child....**mind, body and SPIRIT!** Teach him/her about their Spiritual Parent (GOD) who disciplines, guides, forgives and loves. Teach your child about respect, responsibility and positive roles in developing relationships.

These are the "little things" that I learned that make a "big" difference. I dedicate these notes to my wonderful, grown, handsome, intelligent, awesome, creative, strong, divine Black men John and Jason....*I thank you for the lessons I have learned. You'll always be my precious "babies."*

(1) Your child rises to your expectations. So don't use words like stupid, slow, bad, ugly or "terrible two." Even though your child's behavior today may not be the best, watch your words! You have tremendous power to influence and change your child's behavior. Your words are a gift that build, heal, nurture and motivate your child.

(2) Pace yourself today. If you're feeling tired and overwhelmed, take a "time out for a break" before you have a breakdown. Go for a walk, take a deep breath, read a few pages of your favorite book, put on some uplifting music, delegate duties to others, or just grab your favorite blanket and go take a nap.

(3) Successful parenting is one of the most difficult jobs on the planet. Don't isolate, overwhelm or judge yourself too hard. Talk to other parents, seek help from the elders, read information that empower parents and pat yourself on the back. You're doing a great job!

(4) Call your Mom up today and apologize for all the difficult times you gave her as a child. And then ask her for help with your child. She'll be glad to help. Don't let your ego, pride or distance deprive you of her experience, strength and love.

(5) Once you make a decision….stick with it. Be consistent. Children will test you. They will ask, ask and ask until they get what they want. If you are weak, give in, and not consistent, it's difficult to build trust and respect from your child.

(6) Your child learns from your behavior. They watch more than they listen. If you lose your temper a lot, use inappropriate words and don't cope with difficulties well, your child learns to model that same behavior. Being a parent means you are a teacher and role model too.

(7) Punishment can be verbal, non-verbal or physical. The goal of punishment is to correct and produce positive and permanent appropriate behavior. Reasonable punishment is necessary at times. Just don't punish yourself emotionally by thinking you are a mean parent. Your child needs love, guidance, forgiveness, discipline and reasonable punishment when appropriate.

(8) Instead of rewarding your child's good behavior with cookies, ice cream and candy; begin to give fruit, healthy snacks, privileges or a wonderful hug. And don't forget the same is true for you. Reducing sugar reduces internal stress, hyper activity, tooth decay and mood swings.

(9) Excessive amounts of dairy products, white starches, sugar, ice cream, cheese, and not enough water can create ear infections, asthma, constipation and related problems for your child. Replace fast foods with healthy snacks. There may be resistance at first from your family when you're trying to improve their health, but remember, you're the one who shops and have their heart and health in mind.

(10) "It takes a whole village to raise a child." (African Proverb) That village includes parents, neighbors, church friends, aunties, uncles, coaches, ministers, teachers, store clerks, PTA, your friends, volunteers at camp, law enforcement, librarian, doctors, artists, musicians, etc. Many people will influence your child. As a parent and guardian you not only protect and provide, but also prepare your child how to succeed and survive in the "village."

(11) Keep your self-esteem, sanity and faith strong. You will have good days and then there will be challenging days. Don't lose your temper or lose faith when things go wrong. You can cope better with diapers, crying, demanding schedules, helping with homework, temper tantrums and household chores WHEN you remember to take good care of yourself. Be optimistic and remember "this too shall pass."

(12) Turn off the television and expose your children to different styles of music, art, reading, museums, recreational activities, arts and crafts, dance, interacting with animals, nature, puzzles, games, etc. The television shows "program" your child toward violence, adult themes, undesirable behavior and passive learning. Your child's mind needs to be stimulated by positive influences. Turn off the TV and turn on their minds.

(13) *Mommie, Mama*....these are very precious words. Value and treasure that small precious voice. Be patient and responsive when the voice calls out to you. You are a very important person. You are someone a child can depend upon. You are needed. Soon Mommy becomes MOM. Soon that child becomes a teenager. So enjoy being called *Mommie* now.

(14) Letting your child know that he/she is capable, loved, wanted, unique, protected and important is a way to build healthy self-esteem. The word "family" is derived from the word "familiar." Your child is happier when surrounded by familiar sights, sounds, feelings, experiences, faces and places.

(15) Talk and listen to your child. Make it comfortable for your child to come to you in times of fear or concern. Learn how to handle conflicts in a healthy, loving and mature way. When a parent yells and loses control of their emotions, they lose control of the situation. Children have to learn how to articulate their feelings. They don't always know how to express what they are feeling. Don't be easily frustrated with your child's level of communication. Be motivated to understand, be patient and assist your child in developing positive communication skills.

(16) Teach the "whole" child....mind, body and spirit. Teach him/her about their spiritual parent (GOD) who also disciplines, guides, provides, forgives and loves them. A spiritual foundation is laid in the home and church, not in the schools. The book of Proverbs states, "Train up a child in the way he should go and he will not depart far from it."

(17) Motivate your child to realize their greatness, and natural inner gifts. Affirm their curiosities, explorations, uniqueness and talents. Encourage them to dream, believe in themselves and how to be of service to others. The home is where a child is nurtured, taught about excellence, responsibility, and respect. You can be the best motivator for your child when you are motivated about your own life and possibilities.

(18) Yes, parenting can be frustrating and overwhelming for single parents. But you can do it! Don't give up. You're too blessed to be stressed. Spirit has a way of working things out if you just continue to believe and keep getting up each day to meet the challenge. Take one day at a time and don't let fear, self-doubt or pain from the past consume you. Hold on! Don't expect to breakdown….expect a breakthrough.

(19) Active participation in your child's interest and activities create memories for both of you to remember for years to come. Participation in their sports, creativity, cultural arts, school activities and college planning are vital. A child remembers long into adulthood your involvement and shared joy. It may seem hectic, trivial or too much right now, but it will prove to be rewarding and worth it all.

(20) Your child depends upon you for the intangible gifts more than the gifts you can buy at the store. Remember to give your child the gift of time, listening, discipline, spiritual guidance, forgiveness, consistency, honesty, laughter, family gatherings, reading, cultural pride, storytelling, stimulating their minds with music, dance, poetry, art, crafts, and sports. Teach them how to be wise in handling money, their emotions and the peer pressure. The home is the factory that produces the most important product in the community….a productive and decent human being.

(21) Sometimes your child may test you, resist and disobey you. Be strong and firm. Children need love and boundaries. They are looking up to you to be the stronger and wiser one. Control your emotions and don't lose your temper. Parents don't get discouraged when your child displays resentment or resistance. Determine your boundaries, build bridges of love and communication and hold true to your beliefs. One day they will thank you for showing the love and courage that many children today may not receive. You're doing a great job.

A Parent's Promise
by Jewel Diamond Taylor

I will take time to LISTEN to you.

I will take time to TALK to you.

I will ENCOURAGE you to READ, WRITE
      and develop your personal uniqueness.

I will teach you about your RICH HERITAGE
      to give you roots.

I will guide you in PROBLEM SOLVING and
      LIFE SURVIVAL SKILLS to give you wings.

I will learn to show PATIENCE, FORGIVENESS
      and UNCONDITIONAL LOVE so you will learn to
      feel safe and secure.

I will discover ways to STIMULATE your MIND
      so you won't be bored but motivated to learn.

I will provide DISCIPLINE and GUIDANCE
      so you can make wise choices in your life.

I will offer PRAISE and APPRECIATION
      so you will develop self-esteem.

I will learn to HEAL from my past childhood wounds
      so that I WILL NOT pass my pain onto you.

I promise to teach TRUTH, COOPERATION and SERVICE
to others by my example.

I will teach you RESPECT, HONOR and to GIVE THANKS
to GOD so you will learn to be humble and righteous.

I will seek ways to bring out the BEST IN YOU.

I will teach you about MONEY MANAGEMENT and
PROPER HEALTH CARE so you will NOT BE
dependent on others.

14

WHAT CAN ADULT WOMEN DO TO HELP THE YOUNGER WOMAN-TO-BE?

Because of my association with the African-American Women's Conference on Tour, I have had the honor to meet giving and committed sister-elders who love working with our youth in the community. Emily Gunther and Shquestra Sitawi have been an inspiration and nurturers to thousands of youth because of their high level of creativity, spirituality and empowerment skills. Shquestra Sitawi is an artist, poet, workshop facilitator and an Elder in the Rites of Passage for African-American girls. I asked my sisterfriend to share her comments with you on rites, rituals and initiations for young girls.

SHEQUESTRA SITAWI

In Afrikan tradition, a young girl comes into womanhood through the passing of knowledge and customs. In Zaire, when a young girl has her first menstrual cycle she is immediately secluded from her community and her puberty initiation begins. For up to one month, this child is in isolation with elders being instructed in womanhood on what is expected of women in addition to child rearing and sexuality.

In Gabon, Eshira girls are painted with white powdered clay which symbolizes and ensures strength and good reproductive health as they enter womanhood.

Togo girls have a two part initiation, seclusion and instruction. Zulu's of South Africa and the Ndema of Zambia both seclude their young women. It is during this seclusion that womanhood and adult responsibility are taught in a safe environment.

In America we do NOT have an established program for our girls. We no longer have our ancestral rites and ceremonies. We no longer hear the voices of our ancestors; we tend to turn a deaf ear to the voices in the wind. Young girls need/must have their ritual markings of their passage into womanhood, and because we do not have these ceremonies for our girls, they have developed their own: GANGS, PREMARITAL SEX, DRUGS, etc.

Through rites of passage rituals, "First World" girls learn what it is that the community expects from them. Afrikan children in America also need to know what is expected of them by our community, which can only be accomplished through some type of rites of passage program.

162

All too often in American culture we do not expect anything from our Afrikan children until they are 18 years of age. Then, all of a sudden we expect them to become adults, to act like adults and be responsible like adults without any skills or insight, let alone survive in a country where the dominant culture is racist, or prejudiced against them.

Rites of passage programs give girls a chance to learn what is expected of them by their community. They are given the opportunity to succeed, or fail, in a safe, loving environment with support of elders and peers. The passage program also allows a girl to discover hidden talents, or to showcase that which she has hidden from the world and, often times, from herself.

Through the completion of challenges, a girl begins the process of discovering who she is, and how she fits into the power of being an Afrikan woman. These lessons need to be taught and the rites of passage is one way to do this ritual. If we do not provide rituals for our girls to crossover into the circle of women, they will create their own. Rites, rituals and initiations is what "getting jumped" into a gang is about, as well as body tattoos, and on a more acceptable level, pledging for sororities.

The rites of passage program can eliminate the need for GANGS (artificial family unit), SEX (the need to feel loved), and DRUGS (masking pain). These negative rites of passage rituals are a sign that we as an Afrikan community are not doing our work. We are not passing our knowledge down to our children. We are not giving them their rites, rituals and initiations. As Malidome Patrice Some' states in his book, Of Water And The Spirit, "A person who doesn't get initiated will remain an adolescent for the rest of their life...." Just look around our community....what do you see?

As elder sisters of the community, we are charged with the lives of these young girls, whether we want to accept it or not. Our purpose is to guide them, not instruct them. They already have the knowledge inside; our task is to tap the knowledge and let it flow forth. As elders we are to guide in such a way that the girls feel empowered in all that they do. Now that doesn't mean that every challenge that the girl encounters will be successful, but the outcome can be empowering if handled correctly.

Each of us as Afrikan women have a gift to share with these young women. If you know only how to cook a pot of collard greens, I guarantee there is a young woman out there in our community who needs to know how to prepare greens. If you know only how to clean a house, or iron clothes correctly, I assure you there is someone out there who needs to know how to perform these tasks. There is an art to housekeeping, cooking and child rearing as well as business management and how to be a righteous Afrikan woman.

However, in our desire to compete in the corporate world, many of us were never exposed to this art. I believe if more sisters had been through a rites of passage program, we wouldn't have so many single Afrikan women looking for love in all the wrong places. So I challenge all of you out there who criticize and ostracize the young women and girls seen on the street grasping at Europen straws and looking at eurocentric TV to help them define what an Afrikan woman is, and shall be, to start a rites of passage program.

It doesn't take much. You can just take the young sister who lives next door to you or the young girl who has that lost look in her eyes at your church or sorority and talk to her, and teach her your specialty.

Teach the things that you learned as you set at the kitchen table and listened to your Ma'dear, Nana, Big Mama, Auntie or Grandma talk about life. No matter how skewed it was, it was still a version of the African experience. We must take our children back from the streets, and as Afrikan women we can do it one child at a time. Afrikan women, give your daughters their rites, rituals and initiations....give them their "rites of passage."

165

After experiencing the beauty, joy, insight, bonding, cultural education and spiritual foundation that a rites of passage can offer young teen girls, I, along with the parents of the girls, can see the tremendous value. Young girls benefit in so many ways. They are less prone to repeat some of the mistakes of earlier generations. Their minds, body and spirit are sharpened to make better choices, boost their self-esteem, become culturally aware, prepare for college, sexually responsible, and to honor their bodies, talents and each other.

Today we can see our young sistergirls roaming the malls, watching too much TV, having babies too soon, dropping out of school, feeling isolated on college campuses, living without spiritual joy or morals, giving their personal power away to boys, drugs, peer pressure and depression. Their role models have become the video and musical images that destroy any progress their ancestors fought and died for.

They are too young and immature to know how to ask for a rites of passage or to even know how their future is being denied or destroyed. When adult women provide nurturing opportunities and alternative programs that are preventive measures rather than problem-solving rehabilitation programs....then we become a part of the solution instead a part of the problem.

Wouldn't it be wonderful to see your daughter, niece,

grandchild, or neighbor grow up to be a conscious, spiritual, financially free, healthy, educated, positive thinking, self-reliant and responsible woman? Wouldn't it be satisfying to your soul to know we can break the cycle of women falling into the common trap of mistakes with men, money and the myths of society?

A rites of passage program can be offered in your church, after school, via book clubs, PTA, or within your own family. Our African heritage reminds us, "Each one must teach one."

15

DON'T TAKE GOOD HEALTH FOR GRANTED

Women today are challenged not only with poor childcare, transportation needs and poor education, but also poor health care. The quality of our nation's health care continues to decline because medical professionals are impeded by paperwork, gag orders and law suits. Doctors are given incentives for cost containment which reduces the amount of time spent with each patient. Doctors have become employees of stock holders, CEO's and business management organizations concerned more with the bottom line more than with the caliber of care patients receive. Having health insurance is a luxury. It will guarantee payment of your doctor bill, but it can't guarantee you will be healed, recover or get your money's worth. Therefore, the quality of your health has to be your priority.

Mainstream conventional health care options are drugs, surgery and technology with very little personal interaction.

They exclude compassion and many less expensive proven natural alternatives.

People are either losing faith in traditional medicine, can't afford it, or simply choose a more natural, wholistic approach for health care. You can choose one or the other....or you can integrate the two modalities for the most positive approach.

Males dominate the health care system. Sexism and racism limit our choice of female health doctors and specialists. We must continue to encourage and educate more women to enter the medical/health field. Men don't give birth, menstruate, feel the pain of fibroid tumors, hot flashes, or have pap smears. The lack of sensitivity, few female doctors, awareness and money keep many women of color at home suffering in silence.

The woman who is informed and educated about her physical, spiritual, mental and emotional self is empowered to help herself and her family.

Sisters, the quality of your health is in your hands. Some of us are committing slow suicide with forks, words, attitudes, life-style, procrastination, or lack of knowledge. Ignorance is NOT bliss. What you don't know....can hurt you.

In the previous pages, "financial health" was covered. Now we need to address your "physical health," the condition of your "temple."

Being broke, sick and tired takes up all your time. How do you feel? What is your daily routine for exercise? What anxious thoughts and emotions are creating stress in your neck and back? What foods do you crave? Do you eat "living food" or junk food? Do you drink more alcohol and soda than water? Did you know that water is medicine? Did you know that many women are deficient in iron and calcium? Did you know that many of us suffer from too many surgeries and pain because of poor nutrition?

I love my soul food like most of you reading this book. But even our soul food tends to have too much salt, pork, fat, cholesterol and starch. If you value your "soul's sake," reduce as much as you can. I still enjoy my soul food, but with much more moderation.

Diabetes, asthma, heart problems and cancer are in my family history. My mother passed away from breast cancer and my father passed away from heart and diabetes complications. Yes, I have had my share of health challenges, surgery, pain and fibroid tumors. I've had my 3-minute, low touch, little conversation, no eye contact, prescription giving, insensitive, don't even know my name, no warmth, poor bed-side manner visit at my HMO. I have also had reflexology, iridology, massages, colonics, nutrition counseling, and self study to heal my body.

My family history, experiences and ever increasing self-care awareness have been my motivation for years to improve my diet, decrease intake of sugar, meat, fast foods and to supplement my nutrition by drinking more water, walking, maintaining a positive attitude and taking my herbal supplements (i.e. cascara sagrada, goldenseal, comfrey, calcium, dandelion, spirulina, wheatgrass, bee pollen, black cohosh, wild yam, etc.)

There are many paths to wholeness. Your healing path is your own choice, but please realize your healing rate, quality service, and your right to ask for a female doctor or demand better care from your male doctor are your personal rights.

Take time to read books on your own. For years, I was craving and eating ice like it was candy. I would continually question doctors about the cause. It wasn't until I was in a health food store reading one of the health books that I discovered that ice cravings were called "PICA," a symptom of iron deficiency. Once I started eating more dark green vegetables and taking iron supplements, my craving stopped. The cure was simple. It didn't require a prescription and I was determined to find the answer. "Seek and ye shall find." That is why you want to read more and be committed to your health and healing.

Usually health doesn't become a priority to us until we are really sick. Reading and taking action are usually a reactive response rather than a proactive behavior to keep our bodies vibrant and healthy.

Don't expect your healthcare provider to be totally responsible for your health. Read to empower yourself. Queen Afua from the New York area is the author of "Heal Thyself." It has been my health reference book for years. I highly recommend it for your personal library.

Queen Afua will educate and enlighten you on many subjects such as; prepare yourself and your home; fasting; natural living; detoxification; Afrikan-Caribbean meals; colon therapy, vaginal regeneration; breast-feeding; exercise, massage, yoga; holistic lovemaking, the Canopic Jars; spirituality and more.

As I stated in my previous book **Success Gems**, health is your first wealth." Sisters, start taking positive action to renew and rejuvenate your beautiful temples today.

The first African American woman to be appointed U.S. Surgeon General, Dr. Joycelyn Elders stated in a magazine article: (New Woman, Sept. 1994) *When you've seen as much needless suffering as I have in both my personal and public life, you know the value of prevention. You start to question a health care system that pays for mastectomies, bypass surgery, gunshot wounds and even pediatric intensive care but often not for mammography, papsmears, counseling, family planning and other preventive services.*

173

It is up to you to educate yourself and your family to maintain proper health. Women are the first teachers for the family. Sisters make that commitment to fast, exercise, read more about health, overcome an addiction, eat more fruits and vegetables, and drink more water. When you feel good, you do good! How you feel determines how well you sell, teach, dance, paint, write, parent, supervise, jog, dream, sing, make love, recover from setbacks, or solve problems.

On the average, women live seven years longer than men. You have to prevent and prepare for your future because that is where you will spend the rest of your life. Don't be like some of our elders who say, "If I had known I was going to live this long, I would have taken better care of myself."

16

Save a Sister

Women today are lonely, overwhelmed, depressed, suicidal, sick, in prison, single parents, between relationships, grieving, and fighting addictions.

You may think the sister who looks "so together" is better off than you. Many women, however, are hiding behind masks, choosing negative coping habits or simply can't say, *I need help....I need prayer....I need a ride....I need to talk to someone.*

Whether you call a sister, write a letter, rideshare to the grocery store, sit with her in the doctor's waiting room, visit her in the hospital, pray with her over the phone, or just visit with "no agenda" ....just talk and listen to her....you are being a blessing and will be blessed.

This issue is one of my passions. I know what it's like to lose a loved one and not have the emotional support to see you through the time of funerals and grieving. I know what it's like to be in the hospital or at home just hoping someone would remember you. I know what it's like to feel depressed, lonely and overwhelmed. I know what it's like not to have a car and feel stranded.

I learned to allow others to help me. I've learned the power of "touching and agreeing" with others in affirmative prayer. I've learned to let go of pride, ego and unnecessary pain which allows others to comfort and support me.

Giving is receiving and receiving is giving. It is such a joy to give to others. It is so rewarding to be there emotionally, financially or spiritually for others.

You can learn how to reach out to another sister without allowing her to feel ashamed or alone. But it's also important not to overextend yourself. Some unhealthy people are "drama queens," toxic, irresponsible, not growing from being a victim, or repeating negative behavior patterns. You don't want to fall into an emotional trap of always rescuing that kind of person. Draw your emotional and time boundaries because some people lift and some always lean.

Your support could be needed for sisters caught in a temporary situation or life phase. One day it could be you. Share with her this book or any material that you feel would be uplifting (any books by Iyanla Vanzant, Susan Taylor, Dr. Barbara King). It doesn't take much to make a person feel valued, special, loved and comforted. A little can go a long way.

Usually when someone is "going through" something, they feel like they're the only one who's had that experience. People tend to isolate themselves, choose the wrong coping habits, feel ashamed and even embarrassed because of the confusion, pain or setback in their lives. Because they are overwhelmed and embarrassed, they stay away from the very sources that could uplift them.

Going to church, support groups, and being with family and friends when things are going right is easy. It's during the difficult times they need to stay close to the "well." Unfortunately many choose to sit down, keep it in, stay in and stay away from people and activities that could help to turn the "light" on again during their dark night of the soul. Self-pity or hopelessness sets in with isolation. The ability to see an immediate solution and put the problem in the proper perspective are out of sight and out of mind.

If this describes you at times, you'd be surprised how many around you share common experiences. You are not alone on the physical or spiritual planes of life. The Mighty Comforter and Provider has done it before and He can do it again. Stress, ego, pride, and doubt will cause you to forget that God is able.

Music never fails to lift me during my difficult times. One of gospel's greats, Shirley Caesar, recorded a song that always comes to mind to remind me that God can turn around any situation.

You may not know when
and you may not know how
but He'll do it again.

When our faith is small we want guarantees, details and the estimated delivery time of God's miracles.

These lyrics remind me that when I'm in the valley of despair, I must trust and remember that God has delivered me before with mercy and grace and now I must be patient. There's no need to know how or when. All I need to KNOW NOW in this moment is God will do it again.

Each one can teach one about God's glory and goodness. You will have your own unique testimony and style of comforting someone in pain. Be yourself. Only give what you can and know that is enough. Save a sister or a brother whenever you can.

My intention is to always respond to letters and to listen to my sisters. I have been blessed by many expressions of kindness from my sisters. And I want to be a blessing to others.

"SAVE A SISTER" is part of my outreach ministry. Call or write me. I will "touch and agree with you." Even if my experience, schedule or availability can't be a part of your solution, perhaps I can refer you to someone who can.

Your act of getting up and reaching up is a positive step in the right direction. Even if someone doesn't respond to you right away or give you the answer you want....at least you are not giving in and becoming isolated or paralyzed with fear, guilt, shame or hopelessness. Be motivated enough for your own survival and sanity to reach out to a sister near you. Tap into the energy, resources, network, ministries, and love that is all around you.

17

THE 21ST CENTURY

This book is written just before the turn of the century. And it will be read far into the new millennium. My previous self-help book **Success Gems** and this project are among the new wave of self-help/spiritual/personal development books that are flourishing the shelves of bookstores everywhere.

Knowledge, spirituality and personal development are the keys to our future survival, sanity, and success in the new century. Advanced technology and a global economy have altered values, politics, lifestyles, and world views.

People are desperately seeking satisfaction in their personal and professional lives. The quest for spiritual enlightenment, job satisfaction, security, ending poverty, illiteracy, disease, divorce, racism, sexism, pollution, and violence are on the agenda for the new millennium.

The gap between the "haves" and "have nots" will likely continue to widen. There are obvious indications that disparity between the educated and uneducated, sick and healthy, employed and unemployed, rich and poor, those in darkness and those living in God's light of promise and peace will also continue.

What side of the gap will you be on? The choices you make now, the knowledge you possess, your attitudes, networking, and service to humanity will determine your place in the 21st century. Education, empowerment, enlightenment and economics are the cornerstones of solid foundations.

An ancient Oriental saying warns:
If you want to think ahead one year,
sow a seed.
If you want to think ahead ten years,
plant a tree.
If you want to think ahead one hundred years,
educate the people

We can't afford to forget that "knowledge is power." It's a timeless truth. We must think, love, pray, cleanse, plan, act, and prosper for our children and for future generations to come.

We must devote more time to the people we love rather than the "things and toys" we own. People who believe the popular bumper sticker, "He who dies with the most toys wins" are missing the real essence of life. It should be "The one who lives with the most faith, love, service, wisdom, and courage wins."

Cycles of pain, poverty, ignorance and dependencies need to be broken. When you and I are in debt to someone, a financial institution, a job or the government, the debt becomes a dependency. All dependencies lead to depression and ultimately leads to destruction. As a race of people historically oppressed, we are challenged to grow from being dependent on others for the quality of our lives.

I recall a scene from the movie "Shawshank Redemption." Actor Morgan Freeman played an inmate who had become "institutionalized" after being incarcerated most of his life. Mr. Freeman's character said to another inmate that becoming institutionalized is a process of dependency. *First you hate it, then you get used to it, and then you start to depend on it.*

Men and women are "institutionalized" in many other ways. It can happen in a marriage, a job, an addiction and yes, even our race. At first you may hate the job, the unhappy relationship, drinking alcohol or slavery, but after a while you adapt, tolerate and get used to it. Even when you are given the opportunity or awareness to be free, you can't leave your comfort zone because you have become dependent. You don't know or trust your own personal power to create because we are creatures of habit.

My own ongoing personal transformation to free myself of limitations has lead me to study, pray, grow and share these insights in my books, retreats, Enlightened Circle sessions and lectures.

Hopefully the 21st century will usher in new attitudes. The world needs to come into balance. The female energy, creativity, sensitivities and wisdom need to be utilized and recognized. The balance can reduce the senseless wars, starvation, violence and neglected social conditions.

Next century, optimists hope to see more women involved in the activities and policies that shape the infrastructures of our communities. Women need to rise above the glass ceilings in politics, religion, education, science, healthcare, economics, ecology, media, the arts, businesses, and corporations.

You will need your strong spiritual base to build your family foundation. You will want to be in alignment with your unique purpose, protect your health, have a strong economic base and networking skills.

It will be an exciting time in history. You will be better prepared to withstand the changes and seize the opportunities it will bring by building your foundation with education, empowerment, enlightenment and economics.

As an individual and society, we need to care more about three important relationships to survive and succeed in the 21st century.

1) Relationship with God

2) Relationship with each other (humanity)

3) Relationship to Mother Earth

All three need to be honored, cared for and given respect.

18

Be a conscious sister

Sisterfriends, we can use our voices to talk about the positive and great attributes of our culture, character, children and community. Our voices are the modern day "drum" of yesteryear.

The woman is a major consumer. The forces against our economic, cultural and spiritual growth know how to target us through media and lifestyle marketing strategies. If your mind is negatively programmed to eat, purchase, healthcare, education, childcare, clothing, lifestyle, consumerism, conflict resolution, politics, and Black men, then the well-being of the Black family and social conditions can be influenced because YOU, the nurturer, birth canal of future generations, and con$umer have been programmed how to think, act, feel and believe.

As African-American women, let's be aware and discerning. Let's become conscious consumers, critical thinkers, healers, activists and promoters for the positive in our own communities.

We stand on the shoulders of so many heroes and sheroes. Their legacies remind us that strength, faith, vision, unity and a commitment to our survival and success are necessary to bring about change. No, the "revolution will not be televised" but neither will your evolution. Change begins within each of us....each one teach one.

Every time we contribute to our economic base, uplift one another, open our own businesses, become politically active, heal our families and clean up our communities, we are part of the solution. Every time we put each other down or....take our energy, experience and dollars out of the community....we are part of the problem.

I challenge you and me to seek ways to teach truth, preserve our rich heritage, invest in the future by loving and saving children from despair, and building an economic infrastructure to ensure our stronghold in the future.

Sisterfriends, let's choose wiser in our food selections, mates, careers, values, spending habits, politics, and issues we advocate or tolerate in our community.

SELECTED POEMS

WHEN I COME BACK
by
Jewel Diamond Taylor

In a round table discussion about whether reincarnation was really possible, a financially struggling single woman said, "I want to come back as a rich white woman's poodle that's pampered and rides around all day in her luxury car."

A tired waitress said, "I want to come back rich and make a lot of money and be a mega super recording star."

The frustrated computer tech said, "If I can come back, I want to be the President, so I can change a lot of things about this world near and far."

I sat and thought about it. I said,

"I don't know if it's possible, but if I can....
Lord, please let me come back a BLACK WOMAN.

I want to come back with a mind so fierce and sharp,
with a spiritual faith that never waivers or doubts,
a smile that is warm, with a body divine,
with honey, cinnamon or chocolate skin draped in purple and
gold....and whether young or old....
always have enough money....
so the words "broke," "layaway," "overdue," or
"post dated check" aren't in MY vocabulary.

I want to be a sister to my sister.
A woman wise when choosing my mate or a date.
I want to be able to cook greens, macaroni and cheese,
cornbread, a peach cobbler
and a lemon pound cake all at the same time.

I want to come back a Black woman with self-esteem
worthy of being treated like a Queen from my King.
A woman with patience, love and wisdom for children.
A Black woman with subscriptions to Essence, Jet, Ebony,
Emerge, Black Enterprise, Heart and Soul
and the Wall Street Journal.

I want to come back a Black woman with at least one great
diamond from the Motherland on my finger.
 I want to come back with the quiet courage of Rosa Parks,
the voice of Ella Fitzgerald, the political courage of Ida B.
Wells, the determination of Harriet Tubman, the spiritual
poise of Susan L. Taylor, the business savvy of
Oprah Winfrey, the eloquence of Dr. Maya Angelou and
best-seller books like Terri McMillian and Iyanla Vanzant.

If reincarnation is real, please let me come back as a
BLACK WOMAN!

I'M NOT GIVING MY BLACK BACK

by
Jewel Diamond Taylor

There are some folks I've seen and heard who are ashamed about their color, heritage, history and struggle. I'm glad I know who I am without apology or compromise. I feel empowered, worthy and proud. Our culture is diversified and I know we don't all share the same experiences and sense of cultural pride and joy. Some of us pray to God, Jesus, Allah, Jehovah, Buddha, Jah, or Moses. Our hair textures and skin tones are different. Our taste in music, arts, sports and politics are varied too. Yes, our intellect, dialect and socioeconomic status are just as diverse as other ethnic groups. Yet there are some golden threads that connect us.

The seeds of self-hatred and division that racism and a history of slavery produce must be uprooted. The healing restoration and celebration of African Americans is what I call "cultural esteem." Cultural esteem remembers and rejoices in the victories, struggle, nuances, talent, rituals, strength and richness of a "colorful" people. In spite of all of the injustices, we are still here, we still laugh, we still sing, we create, we teach, we excel, we love our families, our brothers and sisters....and we continue to rise.

Being "Black" is more than a color of skin....it's an attitude and awareness. Those people of color who run, hide, deny or diminish their Blackness inspired me to say and write.... "I'm not giving my Black BACK!"

I'm not giving up greens or grits or saying "girlllll" and putting my hands on my hips.

You see....life for me ain't been no crystal stair and I'm not giving up Rosa Parks, Fannie Lou Hammer, Mary McCleod Bethune, Sojourner Truth, Madame C.J. Walker, Toni Morrison or Dr. Maya Angelou....
cause you see, I am a phenomenal woman.
And I'm not giving my Black back.

I'm not giving up my crown, waves, braids, curls, locks, kinks or kente clothe.

I'm not giving up the Mass Choirs, The Sounds of Blackness, Mahalia, Shirley Caesar, Aretha Franklin or Kirk Franklin.

I'm not giving up sitting in Ma'dear's kitchen eating peach cobbler or sweet potato pie and hearing her ask me, "How you doing baby?"

I'm not giving up going to "you buy, we fry" on Fridays or bar-b-ques on Saturday, playing bid wist or slamming those dominoes.

I'm not giving up Harriet Tubman's train, Soul Train, Coltrane or the midnight train to Georgia.

Oh, no I'm not giving my Black back!

Now you can meet me at the "function at the junction,"
but I still won't give up B.B. King, The Whispers, Fancy Ms.
Nancy, Lena Horne, Motown, the Philadelphia sound or the
Temptations....
'cause you see, it's the way we do the things we do....
like building the pyramids that still stand made from our
forefather's hands
where diamonds, oil, silver and gold are buried
in my rich dark land.
I'm not giving my Black back!
I'm happy being nappy with my wide hips and nose, rich
melanin or just putting lotion on my ashy legs,
oh I'm happy with the skin that I'm in.

I won't deny or forget my ancestors who lay in a wet grave in
the middle passage from slave trade.
And I won't give up on our youth of today who still need a
way made.

I won't give up on Miles, even though he didn't smile.
I won't give back Marvin Gaye, Richard Pryor, Phyllis
Hyman, Billie Holiday, Billy Eckstein, Jackie Robinson or
Jackie Wilson.

I won't give up the electric slide, Alvin Ailey, Bojangles or
Debbie Allen.
You think I'd give up reading my Jet, Essence, Ebony,
Emerge, Black Enterprise, Upscale or Heart and Soul?

For we are a colorful people....like Curtis Mayfield sang,
"we are a people that are darker than blue."

We are honey, cinnamon, mahogany and chocolate.
We are Red Foxx, James Brown, Barry White,
the mothers of the church dress in white, the color purple,
the lady who sings the blues, we are Al Green with
"love and happiness."

Oh no, I'm not giving my Black back....not even Maxine
(Waters), Martin, Medgar, Malcolm, Mandela, Marley,
Marcus, Muhammed Ali or the Million Man March.

I'm not giving my Black back!

Dress for success
by
Jewel Diamond Taylor

Sisters wear beautiful colors so well.
There's a history our fabrics can tell.
Be loyal to your royal past by proudly wearing
your heritage whenever you can.
You should not be commercialized or celebrated during just
Black History month.
The fabrics of kente, mud and golden threads
were designed to drape your hips, shoulders and head.
When you adorn your body and sensual lines
with these regal designs everyone will say that you
look so royal and divine.
Don't be ashamed of your full body and rich hue.
Walk tall and be proud in all that you do.
When you wear clothes that make you feel and look good,
it boosts your self-esteem and appeal.
Your style can put you in a positive mood.
The way you dress says a lot about you
whether purple, gold, red or blue,
braids, curls, jewels, purse or shoes.
Don't let anyone take your smile or crown.
Wherever you step....is holy ground.
Your grooming, image and style make a first impression.
A facial, pedicure, new look and new clothes
can lift you out of a deep depression.

Sisterfriends, Queens and Divas, invest in yourself
Mind, body, spirit, family, wardrobe, health and wealth.

GOD WAS JUST SHOWING OFF WHEN HE MADE YOU

by
Jewel Diamond Taylor

Black women, God was just showing off when He made you.
The Spirit blew precious life into you.
Your body is adored with it's rich hue.
Your round breasts and hips are like the purple mountains
majesty....
        you are Mother Earth.
Your voice gives birth to poems, stories, prayers and song....
        you are the wind.
Your skin was kissed by the sun....
        you are fire.
 The living waters in your belly are from the river Nile....
        you are water.
Your eyes sparkle like diamonds....
        you are minerals.

Divine Spirit guides you in your dreams to pursue.
        You're a radiant diamond from the Motherland.
In spite of life's pressures, you continue to stand.
        Your creativity and faith sustain you to survive.
By your example,
        you teach others how to keep hope alive.

You are caregivers, teachers, leaders and homemakers.
You are artists, students, entrepreneurs and policy makers.

In unity, we are more wiser, richer and strong.
If we "stay in the light"....
      we can't go wrong.

Strength and wisdom....our ancestors continue to send.
So Sistah' Queens....
      let's be loyal to the royal within.

AFTERWORD....

We are part of a cosmic flow that never ceases. Those who live in fear, ignorance and prejudice wish to dominate and suppress the self-knowledge of inner power. Those who choose to believe in their supremacy over other races don't want the oppressed to remember their connection with Mother Earth or God....the Creator of all things....the Great Mystery....the Alpha and the Omega....the omnipresent Power that provides and guides us. Their fear promotes division, greed, violence, poverty and false propaganda.

We must not forget that God is everywhere and in everything. If the rocks didn't exist, your body wouldn't have minerals and you would die. If the sun didn't exist, the plants wouldn't grow and you would die. If water didn't exist, your cells would dry up and you would die. If you feel your strength and power comes from people, a paycheck, your degree or your status, then you'll fail to exist when they no longer exist.

The wise ask nothing of man, they ask all of God.
The mountains speak
The trees sing
A pebble has a soul
The rock has power

When you are aware of your relationship to the earth and to God, you can relax and be carried by the flow of energy called God. You see your interdependent role in all activities and all relationships. You begin to understand and respect the universal laws of cause and effect, reciprocity, attraction, abundance, love, intuition, rhythm, etc. This awareness reduces your fears and desire to control, manipulate or dominate.

Rather than drown in the "mainstream" of stress, conformity, greed, violence, materialism, commercialism, racism, and sexism, there is a "clear stream" of knowledge that can carry you.

The rhythmic Reggae words of the renowned singers, "Third World" tell us....

I've got to raise my conscious high,
so Jah's love can rule the world.
We've got to raise our conscious high,
so Jah's love can rule the world

In order to stop your cycle of pain, victimization, unfullfillment, lack and limitation, become a conscious participator in the divine plan for your life as a co-creator with Spirit. Perceive beyond your five senses and become aware of how to quicken the energy in and around you. There is much to learn about interfacing with the world around you, responding biochemically, emotionally and electromagnetically to the foods you eat, the drugs you take, the emotional moods of the people around you, the dreams and aspirations of your soul, the words you speak, and your belief system.

When you're ready to give up false expectations, illusions of lack, a sense of helplessness and hopelessness, you are on your way to wholeness. The pursuit of knowledge and balance of your multidimensional self **(physical, spiritual, emotional, mental, cosmic)** will offer much reward.

We are challenged to move from fear to faith, from hatred to love, from procrastination to action, from the past to the present, from isolation to participation, from stress to peace, from ignorance to knowledge, from pain to wholeness.

Dear beloved reader, continue reading more and staying on your path of enlightenment. As I stated in the beginning of this book, let's talk more, share more and really encourage each other. Don't let men, hairstyles, petty differences, busy calendars, baditutdes, or religion keep us apart.

I agree with writer Sondra Barnes that "God is too big to fit inside one religion." Spiritual democracy as well as political democracy must be upheld. We cannot afford to judge or alienate someone because of their religion. If you really study religions, the common messages are love, peace, compassion, service, family, faith, and hope.

Find your way home to wholeness. Click your heels three times and remember you will need knowledge, love and courage on your journey. Trust your intuition so you won't be detained any longer. Think on the words of Emerson:

Let man learn that the Highest dwells with him. If he would know what the Great God speaketh, he must go into his closet and shut the door as Jesus said. God will not make Himself manifest to cowards. He must greatly listen to himself withdrawing himself from all the accents of other men's devotions. Even their prayers are hurtful to him, until he has made his own.

This book of messages and insights are my gift to all who are seeking higher ground. I'm thankful to my publisher, contributing writers, family and friends who have supported me in countless ways in this endeavor. I pray my words fall sweetly and gently on your soul. My life's work is devoted to encouraging and motivating people to realize personal, spiritual and professional fulfillment.

I see my reflection in so many like-minded teachers, spiritualists and transformation speakers. I, too, am a devotee of Spirit, simplicity, love and beauty, belonging to no particular sect, believing in a Divine Source of eternally evolving life, "beating the drum" to promote enrichment, empowerment and equality of all people.

Stay in the light,

Jewel

THE BEGINNING

 Appendix

We would like to thank the following writers for their contributions to this book. Feel free to write or call them for additional information:

•Maria Denise Dowd
African American Women on Tour
3914 Murphy Canyon Road, Ste. 216
San Diego, CA   92123
(619) 560-2770
(800) 560-AAWT (2298)

•Cynthia Butler-Hayden, Publisher
Minorities in Business Magazine
4929 Wilshire Blvd., Suite 1060
Los Angeles, CA   90010
(213) 933-0945

•Glinda F. Bridgeforth, author
The Basic Money Management Workbook
8160 Hansom Dr.
Oakland, CA   94605
(888) 430-1820

•Cynthia Brown
Global Destinations Travel
666 5th Ave. #267
New York, NY   10103
(800) 690-3936